The Meditative Path

A Gentle Way to
Awareness, Concentration, and Serenity

The Meditative Path

A Gentle Way to
Awareness, Concentration, and Serenity

John Cianciosi

Quest Books
Theosophical Publishing House

Wheaton, Illinois ◆ Chennai (Madras), India

The Theosophical Society wishes to acknowledge the generous support of The Kern Foundation in the publication of this book.

First Quest Edition 2001

The Theosophical Publishing House

P.O. Box 270

Wheaton, IL 60189-0270

Library of Congress Cataloging-in-Publication Data

Cianciosi, John.
The meditative path: a gentle way to awareness, concentration, and serenity / John Cianciosi.
    p.   cm.
ISBN 0-8356-0796-8
1. Meditation—Buddhism. 2. Spiritual life—Buddhism. I. Title.

BQ5612.C53 2001
294.3'435—dc21   00-068306

6   5   4   3   2   1   *   01 02 03 04 05 06
Printed in the United States of America

To my teacher, the late Venerable Ajahn Chah, whose compassion and wisdom continue to be a source of inspiration for me.

CONTENTS

FOREWORD
by Jack Kornfield

I

T IS A PLEASURE TO INTRODUCE THIS EXCELLENT book to you. In it, John Cianciosi, a Buddhist monk for over twenty years, offers the tools for a wise life, heartfelt teachings gained by his own long training and commitment to inner understanding. John explains with great clarity the teachings and path of Buddhism. He shows us the simple and immediate practices carried by the Tradition of the Elders and by our beloved teacher, Venerable Ajahn Chah. John, like Ajahn Chah before him, makes it clear that meditation and a peaceful heart are not goals for monks and nuns alone, but are available to anyone who sincerely undertakes to follow the path of awakening.

The path must begin where we are. It is easy to see that we are out of balance. We begin our new millennium engulfed in an increasingly speedy and complex world, still fraught with war and conflict. Surrounded by materialism run rampant, with twenty-four-hour commerce and new modern possibilities, we can easily lose our way. For no one with a computer seems to have more free time. Instead, we see ourselves raising hurried children and ourselves caught in the addictions of modern consumer society, perpetuating our human struggles even in the midst of prosperity. Yet the Buddha and the Elders of the forest tradition teach that wherever we are, a life of serenity and wisdom is possible. We can find it in ourselves as a deep human longing, as our own true nature.

How is this done? *The Meditative Path* offers us a way, through the systematic trainings for inner peace that are found in the great monasteries of Asia. It teaches us how to settle the body and skillfully use our breath to calm the mind. It offers guidance on how to work with difficult emotions and thoughts. It shows how pain and conflict can be met with a wise and compassionate heart. It teaches us mindfulness in daily life.

What John offers here is the Buddha's teaching, not as a philosophy, but as a treasury of practices. These are gifts carried by the Elders to help every generation quiet the mind and open the heart. Take them in hand. Read them slowly, and undertake these practices step-by-step. Let them lead you back to your own body, heart, and mind. Let them bring you compassion and peace.

May the teachings offered here bring blessings to all who read.

Jack Kornfield
Spirit Rock Meditation Center
Woodacre, California 94973

PREFACE

M Y AIM IN WRITING THIS BOOK IS TO PROVIDE a comprehensive introduction to the practice of meditation for the serious beginner. However, I am sure that meditators who have been practicing for some time will also find its contents relevant and rewarding.

Although my own background is primarily within the Buddhist tradition, I have found that meditation is a beneficial form of mental development appropriate for everybody. Therefore, I have intentionally avoided using religious terminology that might restrict accessibility to these teachings.

In this respect, I am certain that I am being true to the example of my teacher, Venerable Ajahn Chah, who was a highly revered Buddhist monk and an exceptionally gifted meditation master. Once, a group of European travelers wishing to learn about meditation asked him three questions:

- Why do you practice?

- How do you practice?

- What is the result of your practice?

Seeing that they were sincere and intelligent seekers, my teacher replied with three other questions:

- Why do you eat?

- How do you eat?

- How do you feel after having eaten well?

These answers may seem rather enigmatic, but they were Ajahn Chah's way of stripping away any unnecessary mystery or complexity from meditation practice. Eating is an ordinary process that provides the body with nutrients for physical well-being. Meditation, he was saying, is an equally ordinary mental process that fulfills our inner need for peace and harmony.

This book was written on paper over a very short period of time, but it has been taking shape in my mind for many years. I have been studying, practicing, and teaching meditation for almost thirty years. Within these pages, I have tried to share with you what I have learned on my journey.

When I first encountered Buddhism, I was a restless twenty-three-year-old, eager to see the world, explore different cultures, and experience the rich diversity of life. However, it became clear to me that regardless of where I went or what fascinating new adventure I embarked on, I always took myself along with me and carried as well my personal baggage of unresolved emotions and feelings. I realized that I was, in fact, traveling with a stranger who was neither happy nor at peace. It was then that I started to meditate. I wanted to get to know that unhappy stranger who was me, explore his inner world, and cultivate the well-being that can only come from a mind that is at peace.

I did not find the practice of meditation easy, nor did I see quick results. It is said in Buddhism that there are four types of practitioners. The first is the exceptionally gifted meditator who finds practice easy and achieves results quickly. Next is the practitioner who has a pleasant journey but takes a long time to reach the goal. The third type has a lot of difficulty with the practice but makes quick progress nevertheless. Unfortunately, most of us fall into the fourth category, for whom practice is fraught with hindrances and who progress slowly and only with much patience and commitment.

Of course, we would all like to be in the first group, and maybe you will be one of the fortunate ones. But the slow and difficult journey can be extremely rewarding and enriching. Some of the best meditation teachers I know are ones who had to work through many problems in their own practice. While I may not be a teacher of that caliber, I do feel that my experience with meditation during my many years of contemplative, monastic living has given me a unique understanding of the Meditative Path. Finding myself now as a lay person in the position of teaching this path to other lay people living normal, busy lives, I also appreciate the need to make meditation useful, practical, and relevant for ordinary people.

On my journey I have been blessed with the support, guidance, and inspiring example of wonderful teachers and spiritual friends. For me, Venerable Ajahn Chah was a living embodiment of the fruits of practice—a truly beautiful human being. Ajahn Chah was my spiritual father, and his first Western disciple, Venerable Ajahn Sumedho, has been an older brother who has pulled me up and helped me along on numerous occasions. That this book has been written is mainly due to the compassion and wisdom showered on me by them.

This is not a scholastic work, nor is it a recipe book on meditation techniques. It is a sharing of experience in the belief that it can make your path easier to travel. It presents a gradual unfolding of the meditative process that gently takes you to deeper levels of understanding and experience of meditation. Having read the text in each chapter, I greatly encourage you to practice the recommended meditation exercises, as they will give you a better appreciation of the teachings.

The questions at the end of the chapters reflect actual questions that I have been asked on different occasions over the years. I include them because they help clarify some important points and hopefully provide interesting reading.

In conclusion, this is the type of book I wish I had been given to read when I started to practice meditation. That is why I am offering it to you.

John Cianciosi

CHAPTER ONE

❧❧❧

TURNING ON THE LIGHT

I NTEREST IN MEDITATION IN ITS VARIOUS FORMS HAS
grown dramatically over the last thirty years throughout
the Western world. What started as something of a fad for
alternative-minded seekers who had encountered meditation
during their travels in Asia has come to be regarded quite favor-
ably by a wide cross-section of mainstream society. Meditation
is now being taught in colleges, recommended to patients by
medical practitioners, and even used by basketball coaches to
help players improve their game.

Traditionally, the practice of meditation has been an integral part of spiritual life in many religions. Even today, meditation is often presented within a religious context. While this
approach is perfectly valid and even desirable for those with
religious inclinations, this book will demonstrate that meditation is relevant and accessible to everyone.

Meditation is a systematic, introspective practice to facilitate growth in three main areas:

- *Getting to Know the Mind:* carefully studying our inner world of feelings, thoughts, emotions, and various mental states.

- *Training the Mind:* intentionally cultivating three essential qualities for mental well-being—awareness, concentration, and serenity.

- *Freeing the Mind:* gradually reducing the power of negative tendencies that diminish inner peace and outer harmony.

It is important to note that these three aspects of meditation are not unrelated or separate, but rather constitute a single process of inner exploration, discovery, and development that I call the Meditative Path. There is nothing mysterious, haphazard, or bizarre about this process. It is very logical, and the principles involved can be easily understood in the context of a few basic concepts.

HUMAN BEINGS CAN BE TRAINED

Let us begin by considering the object of our study, the human being—a composite of body and mind. The body is the physical aspect of a human being, while mind refers to everything else that constitutes a person.

A student went to the meditation master and asked, "What is mind?" Without the slightest hesitation, the master replied, "No matter!"

We are all aware of the body and, to some degree, understand how it functions, what its needs are, and how to take care of it. There's nothing mysterious, for example, about using aerobic exercise to enhance one's general fitness, resistance training to build muscle mass and strength, or stretching exercises to increase flexibility. The body can be trained by these techniques to promote good physical health.

The mind can also be trained in various ways. Education is systematic training designed to develop intellectual capacity— the ability to think, reason, remember, plan, and so forth. Meditation is simply another way of training the mind, using various "exercises" to cultivate better mental health and well-being.

GETTING TO KNOW THE MIND

So, meditation is primarily concerned with this thing called mind. But what is mind? For most of us, the mind is a mysterious realm we have not known how to explore. One reason the mind is so mysterious is that it is too close to us. Because we identify so completely with the mind, we are unable to objectify our mental world and observe it carefully. Our experience can be compared to that of a fish in water. The fish is completely surrounded by water, but it is unaware of the water in which it swims. Similarly, though we identify with the mind, we often cannot see its functioning clearly. An ancient Sufi story is very revealing about this human blind spot:

> On one occasion, the Mula Nasruden was outside his house crawling on his hands and knees, searching the ground.
>
> A friend happened to pass by and, on seeing him, asked, "Nasruden, what are you doing in the dirt under this hot sun?"
>
> Nasruden answered without looking up, "I have lost the key to my house, and I am looking for it."
>
> The concerned friend immediately offered his assistance. "Here, let me help you. Where did you lose the key?"
>
> "I lost it inside the house," replied Nasruden.
>
> "But if you lost the key in the house, why are you looking for it out here?"
>
> "Well, it's dark inside the house, so I came out here to search where the light is better."

Only by turning on the light inside his house will Nasruden find the missing key. Similarly, if we wish to understand the nature of the mind, we must turn our attention inward and observe our feelings, thoughts, and emotions. The mental faculty that allows us to observe the mind is awareness, which can be compared to light. While normal light allows us to see external objects, awareness enables us to know our internal mental processes.

THREE ESSENTIAL QUALITIES

I said that meditation involves cultivating three qualities essential to well-being: awareness, concentration, and serenity. Let's take a moment to define these terms, because in order to cultivate them, we must have a fairly good understanding of what they are.

Awareness, which we might also call mindfulness, is the state of "mind being fully present." An aware mind is not just conscious in the ordinary sense, because we can be conscious without being fully aware, without clearly knowing what we are doing, why we are doing it, and what we are feeling. We often move through life with only a modicum of attention to our present experience, operating mainly on automatic pilot and reacting to situations habitually.

However, we do have some awareness, or moments when the mind is fully awake to the present experience. It is important to recognize the subtle, but profound difference between just being conscious and being mindful, or having consciousness with awareness. Have you ever been driving a car when you suddenly think, "Oh! Where am I? I've gone past my turn off!" What was your mind doing before that moment of awareness? You were conscious, but your mind was not fully present—not awake, clear, and mindful.

In meditation, we want to cultivate that fullness of mind that lets us be truly sensitive to the present moment. Stop for a moment and consider, "What am I feeling now? Where is my attention?" Awareness makes this type of introspection and exploration possible. It is an essential element in the practice of meditation, and only through the development of this quality can we cultivate concentration and serenity.

Concentration is the ability to direct and hold our attention on one thing for a desired period of time. If we think of awareness as light, then we might think of concentration as a laser, or focused light. The strength of concentration is determined by how fully we can focus and sustain our attention.

Concentration is the mental counterpart of physical strength. Although we all concentrate to some extent, most of us would agree that the mind is rather unruly, and that it behaves much like a restless monkey, jumping from one thing to another. This unruly mind not only prevents us from applying ourselves fully to a particular task, but it can also make us miserable. Constantly thinking about the past, usually with longing or regret, or the future, often with hope or trepidation, can be oppressive. The mind is in overdrive, and we feel stressed. The need to slow down and develop some mastery over this mental activity is illustrated in the following Buddhist verses:

> More than those who hate you, more than all your enemies, an undisciplined mind does greater harm. Hard it is to train the mind, which goes wherever it likes and does what it wants. But a trained mind brings health and happiness. The wise can direct their thoughts, subtle and elusive, wherever they choose; a trained mind brings health and happiness. (*The Dhammapada*, translated by Eknath Easwaran, 87-88)

Through systematic and gentle effort, we can teach the mind to stop running from one thing to another and to concentrate on one object. But before we can train the mind to concentrate, we must know what the mind is doing. That is the role of awareness. With awareness, we simply know where our attention is at this moment. Even if the attention moves from one object to another, we can still remain aware, because awareness flows, just as a beam of light illumines each object it touches.

However, if we wish to develop concentration, then, in addition to knowing where our attention is, we must also make an effort to sustain our attention on the same object. Every time our attention moves to something else, we need to be aware of that movement and bring it back to the original object. With patient effort and regular training, the mind gradually achieves better concentration. The light of awareness becomes focused into the laser of concentration.

Serenity is an experience of rest, tranquility, even joy. The concentration we are interested in developing through meditation is characterized by serenity and clarity. It is impossible to achieve this type of concentration through sheer force of effort or will power. Forcing the mind to concentrate on a task produces tension, and after only a short time, we may feel exhausted. That is hardly a meditative experience or a desirable state. I can still remember my first driving lesson during which I was concentrating so hard that my head was aching, and I was perspiring all over. I certainly did not feel serene.

Unfortunately, most of us can concentrate only through force or will power. As a result, we often feel like we're jumping between the frying pan and the fire. Either the mind is tormenting us by being the unruly, out-of-control monkey, or we are struggling to pin the monkey down until we're exhausted.

In meditation, we do not force the mind to concentrate. Instead, we try to encourage the mind through vigilant, gentle effort simply to slow down, to be at peace. By means of awareness and patient effort, the mind can be taught to appreciate the pleasant feeling of resting with one object. It will then be happy to remain with that object. Emerging from a period of good meditation, we feel refreshed and serene.

Cultivating the Meditative Path involves developing these three qualities by means of various formal and informal meditation techniques that will be described in the next several chapters. Later, we will explore how these three qualities can be applied to a process of self-discovery that leads to insight, growth, and freedom.

The Meditative Path is not an intellectual preoccupation with abstract concepts; nor is it just a matter of doing a few mental exercises for concentrating the mind. As you will discover, it is a journey marked by thoughtfulness, clarity, and understanding that touches every aspect of your being and your life.

The goal is inner peace and outer harmony. Meditation is the path, and we are all fellow travelers on the journey.

Exercise: Relaxing the Body

As a first step toward meditation practice, try this simple mental exercise for relaxing the body. Relaxation is not so much something you do, but something you allow to happen when you stop tensing your muscles. This exercise is designed to help you release any tension in the body.

Begin by sitting comfortably in a chair or cross-legged on the floor in a quiet place with your eyes closed. If possible, try to maintain an upright posture. Put aside all your concerns for the past and future and just bring your attention to the body, noticing what it feels like to be sitting. Check to see whether the body is balanced and the posture is erect. Try to remain still. Slowly and systematically move your attention to the following parts of the body and be attentive to each area for a short time.

Bring the attention to the area around your face, the forehead, and especially around your eyes. What do these areas feel like? Spend a little time gently releasing any tightness or pressure, relaxing and soothing all the muscles.

Move your attention to the neck and the shoulders, releasing and relaxing all the muscles.

Become aware of your arms, and just let them hang loosely and freely.

Notice the feelings in your hands as you simply allow them to rest.

Bring the attention to your chest, and release any tightness.

Become aware of your abdomen, relaxing all the muscles.

Bring the attention to your left leg, allowing it to be very heavy and completely at rest.

Move the attention to the right leg, and relax it as well.

Now, you can either repeat this process of moving your attention through the body, or just sit for a while, remaining aware of the whole body and being at peace with it.

This exercise can be practiced whenever you like for a period of five to ten minutes. It will help you release physical tension and establish a more peaceful state of mind.

QUESTION TIME

In this section, I will address questions commonly asked about meditation and its application in everyday life.

Is meditation like falling asleep or a dull, fuzzy state of mind?

Quite the contrary. In meditation we cultivate a heightened state of wakefulness and clarity. In fact, dullness is one of the main hindrances to good meditation.

Is meditation the same as relaxation?

Taking time to pay attention to the body and relaxing the muscles is indeed a form of meditation, provided that the mind remains wakeful and alert. A relaxed body facilitates a serene state of mind. However, there is much more to meditation than relaxation.

Is meditation like daydreaming or being lost in thought?

Daydreaming is the very opposite of meditation. In meditation, we try to remain alert and clearly aware of what the mind is doing.

Is meditation similar to hypnosis?

If hypnosis is a state in which you do not have self-awareness and you cannot recollect what you experienced, it is certainly not meditation. In meditation, there should be awareness and a clear memory of the experience.

Will meditation inhibit one's capacity for creative thinking?

No. Creative thinking is the product of a quiet, clear mind. Practicing meditation can facilitate new and meaningful insights.

Is it true that you can cure illness through meditation?

It is a well-known fact that one's state of mind greatly impacts the physical body. Having a peaceful mind, free from the stress of negative thoughts and emotions, is conducive to better physical health. So we can say that through meditation it is possible to prevent or relieve unnecessary physical illness.

Some meditation techniques specifically promote healing. However, I think that it is an overstatement to say that we can cure or prevent all physical illness through meditation.

What about the development of psychic powers through meditation?

Many years ago, I was explaining the basics of meditation to a group of school children. One of the boys seemed quite enthralled as he sat looking at me with big eyes and eager anticipation. Finally, not being able to contain himself any longer, he asked, "Can you really fly?" Of course, he was greatly disappointed when I told him that I was not able to fly without the aid of an airplane.

It is natural for us to have a fascination for the super-normal, and I think it is good to keep an open mind about such phenomenon. In many Eastern meditation traditions, it is firmly believed that meditators who attain very high levels of concentration can develop psychic powers and supernormal abilities. Be that as it may, it is certainly beyond the scope of this book and, more importantly, unlikely to have any practical relevance to our own experience in meditation.

CHAPTER TWO

TAMING THE WILD STALLION

ALTHOUGH THERE ARE MANY DIFFERENT approaches to meditation, using a great variety of techniques, all meditation methods share some basic characteristics and work in similar ways.

The fundamental requirement in meditation is that we find some way to manage the monkey mind so that we can start training it. The best way to tame the unruly monkey is to have an object of attention that acts as an anchor, or point of reference, for the mind. The anchor is called the primary object of attention, or simply the meditation object. Having an anchor facilitates our observation of what the mind is doing and provides a focal point for developing concentration.

To illustrate this point, imagine that you are sitting in a small boat on a very large lake and that there is nothing to be seen on the horizon other than sky and water. Due to wind and current, the boat may drift in one direction or another. However, you would probably not notice the drifting, because there is no fixed point of reference to indicate your position. In contrast, if you dropped an anchor with a rope attached to it, the boat's movement would immediately become apparent.

Similarly, if we try to observe what the mind is doing, it is hard to be aware of the mental activity because we quickly get lost in the ocean of thoughts. When we have an object on which to focus attention, however, we notice when the mind starts drifting away or chasing after one thing or another.

The object that is used as the anchor, or primary object of attention, is what distinguishes one meditation technique from another. One method uses a word or phrase, usually having some spiritual or religious significance, as the meditation object. In Eastern traditions, such a word or phrase is called a *mantra*. The mantra is repeated mentally, vocalized silently, or chanted with careful attention. By gradually replacing all the scattered thinking with this one thought, the meditator achieves a peaceful and concentrated state of mind. Mantra meditation is practiced in many religious traditions, including Buddhism, Christianity, and Hinduism.

The concentrative prayer taught by John Main is an example of this approach. Main learned contemplative meditation from a Hindu guru and later, after becoming a Benedictine

monk, he began teaching a technique of "Christian Meditation."
Brother Wayne Teasdale, who also combines Hindu and
Christian elements in his personal practice, describes the
method as follows:

> Christian Meditation is a mantric form of meditation
> that counsels the perpetual, conscious repetition of the
> mantra from the beginning to the end of the meditation
> period. Like a hammer pounding away at our thoughts,
> the mantra wears away the support system for our false
> selves by replacing each thought with the mantra itself.
> The mantra eventually becomes a vehicle that takes us
> to deeper and deeper states of inner quiet, peace, and
> stillness. (Wayne Teasdale, *The Mystic Heart*, 135)

Teasdale's eloquent description of this type of practice
applies equally well to mantra meditation in any tradition, be it
Christian, Hindu, or Buddhist. What suits the practice to a particular tradition are the words chosen for the mantra. When
Main first started practicing mantra meditation, he used the
word "Jesus" as his meditation focus. Similarly, some Hindu's use
the phrase "Om Shanti," while in the Thai Buddhist tradition,
many meditators use the word "Buddho."

In visualization meditation, another anchoring technique,
we form a mental image and strive to sharpen concentration by

keeping it clear in the mind's eye. The shape and color of the visualized image can range from a simple colored sphere to very elaborate and complex scenes. Once the image has been aroused in the mind, we hold it in consciousness with single-pointed attention, trying to prevent the mind from being distracted by other objects.

In the Tibetan Buddhist system of spiritual training, visualization plays an important role and is used in various ways to develop concentration. Often the meditator visualizes the Buddha or a deity considered to personify some enlightened quality and endeavors to identify so completely with the enlightened being that similar qualities are aroused within the meditator.

Buddhist nun and meditation teacher Kathleen McDonald explains the technique in this way:

> Visualizing deities is made easier by gazing at a picture or statue, then closing your eyes and trying to recall the image in detail. However, this helps you with the details only; don't think your visualized figure should be flat like a drawing or cold and lifeless like a statue. It should be warm, full of life and feeling, three-dimensional and made of pure, radiant light. Feel that you are actually in the presence of a blissful, compassionate, enlightened being. (*How to Meditate*, 113)

Of course, it is also possible to use various physical characteristics of the body, such as sensations, postures, and patterns
of breathing as objects of attention. In fact, we find that in all
meditation traditions, a wide variety of techniques have been
developed around this approach.

All these different techniques are valid and useful because
they work on the same principle: that in order for us to develop concentration and serenity, the mind must stop its restless
jumping and settle down. It is difficult to say which technique
for reaching this goal is better or easier. The fact remains that
each attempts to tame the same monkey—our own mind.

My teacher, Venerable Ajahn Chah, was a highly respected
meditation master, and many people would seek his advice and
instructions. Often people would ask, "What is the easiest meditation?" My teacher would answer, "The easiest way is not to do
it!" Unfortunately, if we take this advice literally, we must continue to live with that unruly monkey, which is not pleasant at
all.

Regardless of what technique we use, it will take time,
patient effort, and personal skill to achieve the desired results of
concentration, clarity, and peace.

THE ANALOGY OF THE WILD STALLION

In Eastern traditions, analogies are often used to illustrate concepts. I have been comparing the untrained mind to a monkey, but in the following analogy, the teachers of old chose a much more powerful animal.

Suppose you wanted to train a wild stallion that has never been broken. First, you would find a very strong post that is firmly anchored into the ground. Then, you would need a long, stout rope, so that you could tie one end around the post and the other end to the stallion. (The wise teachers did not explain how to get the rope around the stallion's neck without being trampled!)

Now that wild stallion, not wanting to be restrained, would try to escape by running this way and that. However, no matter which direction it tried to run, it could only run so far before it came to the end of the rope, where it would have to stop and go back. Eventually the stallion would get tired of running and stand by the post to rest.

The wild stallion represents the untrained mind; the post is the meditation object; and the rope indicates the work of awareness and effort. The stallion resting by the post is like the mind resting in a state of peaceful concentration.

MINDFULNESS OF BREATHING I

The meditation method that we will explore in detail uses

the natural breath as the primary object of attention. Often referred to as "Mindfulness of Breathing," it is one of the most commonly used meditation techniques.

It is important to note that Mindfulness of Breathing meditation is different from techniques of breath control. In the yogic practice of breath control, we intentionally alter the flow and rhythm of the breath. However, in Mindfulness of Breathing, we do not interfere with the breath at all. We just let the body breathe how it wants and when it wants. Our effort is directed at cultivating mental awareness and concentration, rather than teaching the body how to breathe.

There are many good reasons for taking the breath as the object of meditation. To begin with, it is a natural phenomenon that is always present and available to us. Whenever we wish to turn our attention to it, we can immediately know whether the breath is flowing in or flowing out. The breath is a universal and completely neutral human experience. Regardless of your religious beliefs, intelligence, sex, race, or age, if you are alive, you breathe. So everyone can use the breath as an object of attention.

The rhythmic flow of the breath is very calming, and it helps the mind become peaceful. Furthermore, the quality of the breath is closely related to the state of the mind. If the mind becomes more peaceful and quiet, the breath will naturally become more refined. Then, because the object of attention has become subtler, the mind will be encouraged to be even more attentive and calm. Thus, this method can be used to achieve very deep levels of meditation.

As you might expect, even Mindfulness of Breathing is taught and practiced in different ways. Some teachers encourage students to focus attention at the tip of the nose and to know the flow of the breath by the sensation felt as the air passes in and out. Another approach involves keeping the attention at the abdomen, noticing the rising and falling motion resulting from the in and out flow of the breath. Others prefer to follow the path of the breath, experiencing the inhalation from the tip of the nose to the chest and down into the abdomen. The exhalation is then followed in reverse order.

Being mindful of the breath by any of these means will work if we can develop the required skill. However, I feel that trying to know the breath by being aware of a specific physical sensation often creates an unnecessary difficulty. Whether it is the sensation at the tip of the nose or the abdomen, the object will not always be clear to the mind. New meditators often experience the frustration of not being able to "find" the meditation object because they cannot feel the breath at the tip of the nose. This presents an unnecessary obstacle.

However, if I ask you, "Are you breathing in or are you breathing out?" you immediately know the answer. You do not have to search for any particular sensation to let you know that you are breathing in or out. Any time you wish to know the breath, you can do so by arousing the awareness that knows whether the breath is coming in or going out. So, the object of meditation is always directly available to the mind. It is just "knowing the breath" as it flows in and out.

KNOWING THE IN BREATH AND OUT BREATH

The first stage in the practice of Mindfulness of Breathing is simply knowing whether the breath is coming in or going out. It is as if we stop at a railway crossing and notice whether the passing train is coming from the west going east, or coming from the east going west.

During the meditation, we establish our attention on the in and out breath and encourage the mind to relax with the breath. However, we do not expect the mind to remain focused on the breath. It will want to think about this and that, jumping about as usual. At this stage, our main objective is to sharpen the power of awareness. When the mind is with the breath, we know it. If the mind is not being attentive to the breath, what is it doing? It is important to remain alert and watchful. Each time the mind wanders off, we gently but firmly bring the attention back to the breath.

Because the mind will still want to monkey around, we have to be patient and give it some rope. It is not a matter of fighting or struggling with the mind, but a process of teaching the mind, continually encouraging it to abandon all other activity and return to the breath.

COUNTING THE BREATH

To help keep the attention on the breath, I often suggest one of the following aids:

- Mentally noting "In" with each inhalation and "Out" with each exhalation.

- Mentally counting the breath. At the end of the in breath, make a mental note "one." At the end of the out breath, again note "one." At the end of the next in breath and out breath, note "two". . . "two," then "three". . . "three," and so forth, until you reach "ten" . . . "ten." Then start again at "one." If at any time you lose count, simply start over with "one" . . . "one."

Counting the breath serves two purposes. First, it provides the mind with something of a challenge that encourages it to remain attentive. Second, it helps us know how attentive the

mind is. If we continually lose count, we'll know that the awareness is still weak and the effort too slack.

Using either of these aids is optional. You may want to
experiment with them to see whether they are helpful in your
practice. However, remember that the breath is still the primary object of attention. These aids are like crutches that you can
use when necessary.

RIGHT EFFORT

Referring to the analogy of the wild stallion, you can appreciate the importance of having the right length and strength of
rope. If the rope is too short, the stallion may injure itself in
attempting to escape. If the rope is too weak, it will not be able
to restrain the stallion.

Similarly, if during the meditation we try to force the mind
too much, we will create tension and probably end up with a
headache. It is not possible to strangle the mind into a peaceful
state. On the other hand, if we are not vigilant in guiding the
attention to the meditation object, the mind will never learn to
concentrate. Hence, we must discover the balance of right
effort through trial and error.

As an example of right effort, consider a mother looking
after a small child. The mother gives the child a toy and tells
him to play with it. The child plays with the toy for a brief time

but soon becomes bored and starts looking for something else to do, like reaching for the computer keyboard or the cup of coffee on the table. Now, a good mother knows that this is how children behave, so she remains watchful. Every time the child wanders away, she patiently brings him back and encourages him to play with the toy. If the mother is careless and ignores the child, there may be unfortunate consequences. An equally unsatisfactory outcome would result if the mother were to lose her temper and start screaming at the child because he will not be still.

When training the mind, we must learn to act like good mothers.

PREPARING FOR MEDITATION

The process of meditation is one of gradually calming down, collecting ourselves, and settling into the present moment. It is not possible to change gears suddenly from our normal fast pace of living to a meditative state without some preliminary preparation. To facilitate the transition, it is helpful to establish a few conducive external conditions.

Time

There is no one time that is best for meditation. We are all different and so must discover our own best time. However, there are some guidelines for choosing a suitable time.

You cannot rush into a period of meditation in the same way you might rush to a coffee break. It is important to slow down before you begin the meditation. If you have been very busy, you may want to take a little time to unwind by doing some stretching exercises, going for a relaxing walk, or taking a shower.

Try to choose a time when you are physically comfortable, that is, not too hungry, too full, too tired, too hot, or too cold. Unfortunately, most busy working people with families have very limited options when it comes to choosing a time for meditation. So it is important to make the best of what is available.

While on the subject of time, it may be appropriate to discuss the length of time for each meditation period. Again, this depends on the individual. An experienced person may easily meditate for an hour or longer. However, I recommend that beginners start with a ten- or fifteen-minute period. As you become more comfortable with the practice, you can gradually increase the time. Having decided on the length of time for meditation, you may find it helpful to set a timer, freeing yourself from the need to look at a clock.

Needless to say, frequency and regularity of practice are very important. Meditating once or twice a day on a regular basis makes it possible to build up momentum. Irregular or occasional practice may still be beneficial, but it will not be as effective in developing the necessary skills.

Posture

Although meditation is a mental process, we cannot completely ignore physical posture, because the state of the body affects the mind to some extent. For this reason, there are guidelines for what constitutes correct posture in meditation. However, do not allow these "rules" to hinder your endeavor. If you cannot sit in the correct posture, just practice in whatever posture is suitable for you.

When most people think of meditation, they imagine a yogi sitting cross-legged on the floor. Indeed, the cross-legged yoga posture, either half-lotus or full-lotus, is the traditional meditation posture used in the East. It is a very stable and comfortable posture for those adept at it. Unfortunately, most Westerners find it difficult to sit cross-legged without a lot of discomfort. If you wish to sit in this way, it may be advisable to practice yoga or other stretching exercises in order to increase your flexibility. Also, sitting on a firm cushion will reduce pressure on the legs and help you sit erect.

Of course, you can also meditate sitting in a chair. The chair should be of a suitable height so that your feet can rest on the floor while you are sitting comfortably upright.

Correct posture sends the right message to the mind. Regardless of whether we are sitting cross-legged or on a chair, we want the body language to say to the mind, "Be peaceful, but stay focused and alert." Thus, it is best to sit in a comfortable position remaining quite still. The back should be erect, with the top of the head reaching toward the ceiling.

A more detailed description of the posture is given in the exercise below.

Place and Clothing

Find a quiet place in your home or in an outdoor setting where you are least likely to be distracted by noise or people. At first this may be a challenge, but with planning and creativity you can arrange space to meet your preferences and need for privacy. Clothing for meditation should be loose fitting and comfortable, as this allows you to relax more easily.

EXERCISE: SITTING MEDITATION

Find a reasonably quiet and private place. Sit in a position that feels comfortable so that you can remain still for ten or fifteen minutes without experiencing a lot of pain. You can either sit on a chair or cross-legged on the floor.

Try to keep your back erect. This is best achieved by pushing the lower back forward and allowing the abdomen to relax. The rest of the back follows the natural shape of the spine. Keep the neck straight and the top of the head toward the ceiling. Let the shoulders hang down and keep the arms loosely by your sides. Rest your hands one on top of the other in your lap or as you find comfortable.

Close your eyes and your mouth, but keep your teeth slightly apart. Let the body breathe naturally through the nose. If for any reason you cannot breathe through your nose, just breathe through the mouth.

Now, in order to achieve peace and concentration, it is essential that you intentionally put aside all concern for other matters. For this brief period of time, you are not interested in memories of the past or plans for the future. You are taking time out from all your responsibilities at home and work. When thoughts about any of these things come into the mind, just let them go. You are not interested, because this is your time to rest.

Leaving everything and everyone outside, bring your attention inward. Come within, and experience the body sitting. Let the mind sink into the body and sit with the body. What does it feel like? Is the posture balanced? Is the body erect? Is the body still? Spend a little time caring for the body by systematically moving the attention through the body, gently relaxing the different parts as explained in the exercise of the previous chapter.

You are now sitting quite still, the body is relaxed, and the mind is sitting with the body. Now, become aware of the breathing. Let the body breathe as it wants, but try to sustain the awareness that simply knows the breath coming in and the breath going out. Encourage the mind to relax with the breath—peacefully breathing in, peacefully breathing out. You may want to count the breath to help the mind remain attentive.

Try to allow everything else to fade into the background as you continually arouse interest in the flow of the breath. Only breathing in, only breathing out. If your mind drifts away to something else, just note this fact, and gently but firmly bring the attention back to the breath. Continue in this way with patient and vigilant effort.

When it is time to end the meditation, stop concentrating on the breathing and allow your attention to rest with the body once again. Be at peace with the body. Sit quietly for a few seconds, at peace with the surroundings, and then stretch your legs and open your eyes.

Try to practice this meditation exercise for approximately fifteen minutes, once a day. Gradually, you will develop the skill of calming and concentrating the mind.

QUESTION TIME

Let us now address some questions that are often raised by new meditators.

Should I meditate at the same time each day?

There are some advantages to having a regular time for your meditation. Both the mind and body seem to respond well to regular patterns. As the mind becomes accustomed to meditating at a particular time, it will naturally incline towards a meditative mood at that time. Having a regular schedule also makes it more likely that you will do the meditation.

However, it is far more important to meditate on a daily basis, regardless of whether it is at the same time or not.

Can I meditate with my eyes open?

Yes, it is possible to meditate keeping your eyes partly
open; in fact, this is how they meditate in the Zen tradition. I prefer the more common approach of meditating with the eyes gently closed, because it removes the
distraction of visual objects and makes it easier to focus
attention on the meditation object.

Is it possible to meditate lying down?

In theory, we can meditate in any posture, but in practice, some postures are more suitable than others. Lying
down is a very comfortable posture. Unfortunately, it
gives the wrong message to the mind. It tells the mind,
"Relax, take it easy, go to sleep," and that is usually what
happens; we fall asleep. While lying down is a good
posture for relaxation, it does not promote the alert and
clear state of mind required in meditation.

However, if for any reason you are unable to sit up,
or need to remain in a reclining posture, then by all
means meditate while lying down. For example, if you
are ill and confined to bed, it can be very beneficial to
do some meditation. Being attentive to the breath and

gently calming the mind will not only make the discomfort of sickness more bearable, but it can also promote the healing process. In later chapters we explore
the power of the mind to influence the body and see
that a peaceful mind is indeed conducive to physical
well-being.

*When I pay attention to the breathing, it feels like I am controlling it. Is this
normal?*

When new meditators first start practicing Mindfulness
of Breathing, they often find that simply by being
attentive to the breath, they unintentionally interfere
with its flow. The breathing becomes somewhat unnatural and may feel uncomfortable, possibly causing
tightness around the chest. This common experience
should not be a cause for undue concern. However, it is
necessary to understand what is happening so that you
can deal with it appropriately.

It is difficult for most of us to simply observe something without interfering with it. But we can, and need
to, develop this ability. So, during the meditation, regularly remind yourself to allow the body to breathe as
it wants and when it wants. With practice, as you

become more familiar with this technique of meditation, you will find yourself settling back and relaxing into a role of being an interested, but unbiased observer. The breathing will find its own rhythm, according to the needs of the body, and you will feel comfortable.

Achieving this state of being physically comfortable and at ease with the breath while meditating is important. Otherwise, it will be difficult for you to meditate for very long or develop more refined meditation states. The situation may be compared to exercising on a treadmill. Fast walking or running on a treadmill is an excellent form of exercise for developing general fitness and stamina. However, before you can walk quickly or run, you must first learn to feel comfortable and relaxed while walking on the treadmill at a normal pace.

Should I analyze the thoughts that come into my mind during meditation?

At this stage of training, the mind is still very noisy with many thoughts about all sorts of things. Most of this mental activity is just habitual recycling, because the mind has not yet learned to rest in silence and peace. Generally, these thoughts have no special significance and require no special attention. When thoughts come into the mind, just recognize them as thinking, planning, remembering, and so forth and let them go. Continually bring your attention back to the breath.

If something comes up that you feel is important, make a mental resolve to deal with it after the meditation period and continue the meditation. Later we will discuss the practice of contemplation and reflection, which involves careful and systematic investigation of mental states and emotions. However, before we can embark on that practice, it is important to first establish a good foundation of awareness and concentration. We need to thin out the jungle of thoughts so that we can begin to see clearly.

I don't normally have so many thoughts, but when I sit in meditation, it's like opening a can of worms. Where do all these thoughts come from?

Usually we keep the mind preoccupied with a lot of sensory stimulation and mental activity. The mind is accustomed to being busy, but during meditation we are trying to keep the mind occupied with only one simple object, the in and out breath. It is to be expected that the mind, not used to such simplicity, will start grasping at this thought or that memory out of restlessness and boredom. However, once the mind experiences the joy of resting in silence, it will no longer behave in this way.

Is it possible to do too much meditation?

This is not a common problem, but it is important to pace yourself according to your ability. If you intend to do a lot of meditation, such as on a meditation retreat, I would recommend doing so with the guidance of an experienced teacher.

.

CHAPTER THREE

LIKE A BABY
LEARNING TO WALK

I N THE LAST CHAPTER, I INTRODUCED THE PRACTICE
of Mindfulness of Breathing and encouraged you to try a
meditation exercise using that method. Now that you've
had some experience with this method, it may be helpful to
examine some of the common observations made by new meditators and consider how to further develop your practice. This
discussion will then lead us into exploring the next stage of
Mindfulness of Breathing, in which we establish a more refined
level of attention on the breath.

Having already taken a few steps on the journey of introspection and mental cultivation, you may have realized that
understanding the theory of meditation is not the same as being
able to do it. The theory is relatively simple to comprehend, but

developing the practical skill requires much training and a great deal of patience.

I usually discourage students from thinking about meditation in terms of success or failure. It is far better to regard the time we spend practicing as a learning process. Every meditation period can teach us a little more about the mind: its strengths and weaknesses, its tendencies and habits. Only with the knowledge that comes from observation and experience can we achieve the goals of meditation outlined in Chapter 1. Thus, my teacher would often say that the only unsuccessful meditation is the one that we failed to do, because then we did not learn anything.

Consider the experience of a baby learning to walk. How many times does a baby try to stand and take a step, only to fall down again? If the baby started thinking about how difficult it was to walk, she would probably stop trying. Fortunately, babies do not think like that, so most babies learn to walk and eventually to run. I am sure we are all glad that, as babies, we kept getting up each time we fell down.

Let us look at the usual experience of a "baby meditator" taking those first steps.

THE BEHAVIOR OF THE MIND DURING MEDITATION

Initial attempts at meditation are a rude awakening to many

people. Often they are shocked to discover that their minds have so little focus and attention. However, becoming aware of this fact is, in itself, a wonderful revelation and an important first step in getting to know the mind. Do not be disappointed if the experience is not what you expected or hoped for. Instead, carefully consider what you did experience during the meditation and how the mind behaved when you tried to remain mindful of the breath.

You probably observed two very common habits that the mind exhibits during meditation. First, you may have noticed that quite frequently the mind forgets the breath completely and gets lost in some other activity for a while. During this time, the mind is preoccupied with thoughts or sensory experience, or just drifts from one thing to another, without clear awareness. At such times, you do not even know that the mind has forgotten the breath, nor do you know what "monkey business" the mind is up to. This common occurence can be considered a lapse in mindfulness during meditation.

Then, inevitably there arises a new moment of awareness, an instant when you realize that the mind has indeed wandered away from the breath. The experience is like waking up and becoming fully present again. It is important to embrace this moment of awareness by noting clearly what the mind is doing and, without irritation, disappointment, or discouragement, gently but firmly return your attention to the breath.

At this stage in the practice, we do not expect the mind to concentrate fully on the breath. We know that it will wander off, so the challenge is to notice when the mind drifts away and where it goes. Our primary concern is to sharpen and strengthen the faculty of awareness that allows us to notice these movements.

With regular practice, your meditation will gain momentum. As you develop greater skill, you will find that the frequency and duration of the lapses in awareness gradually decrease. My teacher compared this learning process to a dripping faucet. Each drip represents a moment of awareness. At first, the faucet drips only sporadically with long gaps between drips. Gradually, the drips become more frequent until there is no gap between drips, and the water flows in a stream. Similarly, at the beginning of meditation, the moments of awareness may seem few and far between, but with practice, the drips eventually form a stream, and we experience the wonder of being truly awake.

The second observation you will have made is that the mind seems capable of doing a number of things at the same time. While you continue to know the in and out breaths, the mind is also thinking, hearing, feeling sensations in the body, and so forth. In reality, the mind can be conscious of only one experience at any given moment. However, the mind is extremely fast, and consciousness moves from one experience to another with such speed that it gives the impression of simultaneous perception of different objects.

In contrast to the speed of consciousness, a physical process, such as breathing, is very slow. In the time it takes an inhalation to flow in, the mind can think numerous thoughts and process a great deal of information. Thus, although we may still know that the breath is flowing in, during those moments when the mind is thinking and hearing, we are not truly attentive to the breath.

As long as the attention on the breath remains somewhat superficial, we may continue to have a lot of mental activity, even while successfully counting the breath from one to ten. Our task is to gradually thin out extraneous mental activity by continually encouraging the mind to be interested in the breath rather than in other things. The process is a bit like being in the midst of a group of people who are all talking. If we are really interested in hearing a particular person in the group, we can focus our attention almost exclusively on what that person is saying while disregarding all the others.

In summary, we can say that in the first type of experience, in which the mind completely forgets the breath, there is a lapse of awareness for a period of time. In the second, where the mind seems capable of doing a number of things at once, there is awareness, but attention is not yet focused.

HELPFUL ATTITUDES IN MEDITATION

How should we continue at this stage? Needless to say, practice improves with patient effort. However, it is obvious that the way we view or approach any undertaking greatly influences the experience and the outcome. With the appropriate attitude, we will find it easier to sharpen awareness and strengthen concentration, resulting in a more peaceful meditation experience. Therefore, I greatly encourage fostering three mental attitudes helpful in the practice of meditation: interest, carefulness, and contentment.

Arousing Interest

If we can arouse interest in the meditation object, in this case the breath, the mind will automatically remain attentive to it and become focused more easily.

Now, is the natural breath interesting? New meditators often complain that the breath is "so boring." The reality is not that the breath is boring, but rather that we are bored. There is nothing in this world that is intrinsically interesting or boring. There are only interested minds and bored minds. The interest

does not come from the object; it comes from the mind per-
ceiving that object. If this were not the case, then everyone
would be interested in exactly the same things. But because
interest comes from the perceiver, anything can be interesting,
and everything can be boring.

In meditation, we want to develop inner strength and self-
empowerment. We are striving to train the mind so that we can
focus attention on the object we choose at the time we desire.
This means that we are not just waiting passively for some fascinating and exciting thing to grasp our attention. Rather, we
are actively generating interest from within ourselves. Self-
empowerment means that we stop being the monkey whose
attention is drawn by whatever bright object comes into view
and take hold of the freedom we have to arouse interest in the
task at hand.

To help stimulate interest in the breath, you may want to
contemplate the fact that life and the act of breathing are insep-
arable. Since taking the first breath at birth, each exhalation has
been followed by an inhalation. But, one day there will be an
exhalation and . . . nothing. No inhalation. Moreover, we never
know which breath this last one is going to be. Now, this
thought is not intended to frighten you or to cause anxiety, but
simply to arouse interest in that next breath through the realization that each breath is indeed precious.

Carefulness

The ability to pay careful attention is very much the same as being able to concentrate. Consider the degree of carefulness a neurosurgeon needs to have when performing an operation. If we can arouse the same quality of carefulness while being attentive to the breath, the mind will have little time for distractions. Being carefully attentive to the breath means that we care about it. Caring allows us to experience each breath more fully, for a longer time without distraction.

Contentment

Being contented with the present moment is indeed a blessing. Contentment allows us to experience the moment fully, and it is therefore a prerequisite for mindfulness. Do not confuse contentment with complacency. Complacency implies disinterested laziness, while contentment is the ability to abide in the present, free from the compulsive habit of always wanting something else.

If we can establish an attitude of contentment during meditation, the mind will be more willing to remain with the breath and less inclined to chase after distracting thoughts. It will be easy to let go of or relinquish concern for the past and the future, to put aside everything else, and to embrace only the experience of one breath at a time.

Practicing Mindfulness of Breathing with these attitudes will greatly facilitate progress by sharpening awareness and strengthening concentration. The mind will become more peaceful and reach a deeper level of meditation.

MINDFULNESS OF BREATHING II

As described in the last chapter, the first stage in Mindfulness of Breathing is simply to know whether the breath is coming in or going out. I referred to this stage as "knowing the in and out breath."

At this level of awareness, our experience of the breath remains superficial and sporadic. However, if we continue to practice on a regular basis, making an effort to sharpen awareness by using the skillful means described above, then the mind will naturally experience the breath in more detail. Thus, the meditation becomes deeper, and we gradually arrive at the second stage in the practice of Mindfulness of Breathing.

Before we go further, it is important to understand that the terms "first" and "second" stage do not refer to separate steps in the practice. It is not that you practice stage one for a week or month and then decide to move on to stage two. These terms are used only as markers to indicate a gradual progress in the process of being increasingly attentive to the breath. There is no clear-cut demarcation between stage one and stage two; nor do you intentionally move from one stage to the other. Rather, you experience these stages as a natural progression that results from skillful training of the mind.

Have you ever been to the beach and walked slowly out into the sea? As you walk in, the water gradually covers your feet, ankles, knees, waist, and so forth, until you are completely immersed. We can think of progress in meditation as being a similar experience: a gradual immersion into the sea of serenity as the mind becomes increasingly attentive to the meditation object.

Metaphorically, we "walk into the breath" by observing the breath more carefully and with more interest. We then notice that the rhythmic flow of the breath is not an unchanging process. The quality, feel, and character of the breath changes according to the needs of the body. Sometimes the breath flows slowly, taking a long time to come in and go out; at other times, the breath is rather short, coming in and going out more quickly.

It is important to remember that we are not intentionally interfering with the breath or altering its natural flow. The body continues to breathe as it wants. We are simply paying more careful attention to the breath, thereby observing it in greater detail.

These observations bring us to the second stage of Mindfulness of Breathing, which I call "knowing the long and short breath."

Knowing the Long and Short Breath

The terms "long" and "short" refer to whether the breath takes a long time to flow in and out, or only a short time. These terms do not have any independent significance and are only meant to indicate the relative changes that naturally occur in our breathing. In other words, an in breath is only long in relation to another in breath that was shorter and vice versa.

Going back to the example of watching a passing train, at the first stage of observation, we are aware only of the fact that the train is coming from the west going east, or coming from the east going west. But at this stage, we are more attentive and take greater interest in the train. Not only do we notice the direction of the train, but we also know whether it is a long train or a short train.

DEEPENING YOUR EXPERIENCE IN MEDITATION

In order to deepen your meditation experience, continue practicing Mindfulness of Breathing on a regular basis according to the exercise given in the last chapter. If you are feeling comfortable meditating for fifteen minutes, you may want to lengthen the time of your meditation by five minutes or so. However, the quality of your effort is more important than the duration of the meditation period.

Try to be attentive to each breath, continually encouraging the mind to let go of, abandon, and relinquish all other activities. Learn to be content with the experience of one breath at a time. Consider each breath as precious, as though it could be your last. When the breath goes out, remain attentive: will it come back in?

By practicing in this way, your mind will incline towards the breath more easily and remain attentive to it longer. You will observe the nature of the breath in greater detail, noticing what the breath feels like: whether it is long and slow, or short and quick. With this increased level of awareness and concentration comes a deeper meditation experience. The amount of mental dialogue and activity will gradually diminish and the mind will become increasingly quiet and peaceful.

A WORD OF CAUTION REGARDING PROGRESS

Having introduced the notion of progress in meditation, it may be valuable to conclude this chapter with a word of caution.

Generally speaking, we can say that if the practitioner is experiencing a greater degree of comfort, peace, and clarity during meditation, then the practice is going in the right direction. However, there is no way of knowing how fast or slow, with what ease or difficulty any of us will progress along this path.

Each of us brings a unique set of attributes, both positive and negative, to the practice of meditation. If you have accumulated a lot of careless and frenetic mental habits (welcome to the club!), it may take considerable training to achieve a peaceful state of concentration. On the other hand, those who have calm, clear, and disciplined minds to begin with may find the process easy from the start. Needless to say, you can only start from where you are, but do start!

It is also worth remembering that there are many ups and downs in the practice of meditation. Training the mind is not a simple and smooth progression towards ever deepening levels of meditation. Sometimes the experience can be like taking one step forward and two steps back. Obviously the meditation will be greatly affected by your mental and emotional moods as well as the physical state of the body. For instance, if you have just received some bad news or are ill with the flu, it will not be easy to concentrate the mind on your breathing.

Finally, I usually discourage meditators from being overly concerned with the notion of progress. This is because such a preoccupation can become a distraction for the mind, preventing it from achieving calmness and concentration. Naturally, you will wish to make progress; however, having established that aspiration, you should simply get on with the practice, patiently creating the right conditions. The results will come naturally.

QUESTION TIME

Why is it that, when I meditate on the breath, I often feel tension in my eyes, as if I were staring at something?

It may be that you are trying to focus the mind on the breathing with too much effort. Try spending a little more time relaxing the muscles in your face before turning your attention to the breath. Also, while practicing Mindfulness of Breathing, encourage the mind to sink into the breath and relax with its rhythmic flow.

Avoid forcing the mind too much; give it some "rope." Rather than just trying to concentrate on the breath, put more emphasis on noticing the movements of the mind. Only after awareness has been well established will it be possible to make greater effort to strengthen concentration.

It is useful to remember that, while training the mind in meditation, we try to emulate the attitude of a caring mother rather than that of a harsh prison warden.

Can I have music playing during meditation?

When practicing Mindfulness of Breathing, it is usually best to meditate in a quiet place without distracting noise or music. This will make it easier for the mind to remain attentive to the breath. However, playing soft, tranquil, and unobtrusive background music may help you calm down and achieve a meditative mood more easily. Soft music may also act like "white noise" that helps to blunt the effects of other sounds. You may wish to experiment with this option. However, remember that there is nothing more peaceful than the sound of silence.

While meditating, I see different colors in my mind. How should I react to this experience?

Unlike the perception of light that many meditators experience when they attain deep concentration, the appearance of colors or images in the early stages of meditation is mainly due to the proliferation of an active mind. If you are practicing Mindfulness of Breathing, you treat such images in the same way as thoughts, sounds, or sensations. Simply recognize them when they come into consciousness and let them go, continually encouraging the mind to return to the breath.

As a general rule, it is best to consider the various perceptions that arise in the mind during meditation as "visitors" passing through. Neither become infatuated and led into distraction by the visitors, nor fight to get rid of them.

Is it true that I should choose a meditation method that is compatible with my character type?

There is an element of truth in this view, because you may find practicing one particular method a little easier than another. However, of far greater importance than the method used is the way in which it is practiced. In other words, you must gradually discover the most effective approach to guide and teach the mind in order to achieve clarity and concentration.

Depending on your temperament and mental tendencies, you may need to adapt the approach regardless of the method being used. For instance, if you tend to be very rigid, stern, and controlling, you need to be wary of using too much force in the meditation practice. A more relaxed approach may be more effective. On the other hand, if you are very casual and easygoing, you may need to be a little more strict and firm with the mind when training it in meditation.

Through practice and careful observation, you will begin to understand the tendencies of your mind and thus be able to fine tune the approach so as to achieve the desired results.

When I play a computer game, I become completely focused on the game. I don't hear the people around me, and time seems to pass very quickly. Is that like a meditation state? And why doesn't the same thing happen when I practice Mindfulness of Breathing?

It is quite easy to become absorbed in things we find interesting and exciting. When we become absorbed in that object of attention, the mind is indeed in a concentrated state. However, this type of concentration is not usually accompanied by the qualities of awareness and serenity and is not, therefore,the same as a meditative state.

While reading an absorbing novel or watching a captivating movie, we can easily become so involved in the experience that we lose track of time and our surroundings. But the mind is by no means peaceful and clear during that time, nor do we feel refreshed and clearheaded afterwards.

No, I am sorry to say that we cannot achieve the lofty goals of meditation by these means of escape. In fact, you will usually find it much more difficult to meditate after being absorbed in such a way, because the mind will be even more cluttered than normal. Have you noticed how your mind is full of images, memories, and dialogue for quite some time after watching a movie? A stimulated mind makes it very difficult to practice Mindfulness of Breathing.

Of course, there are occasions in ordinary life when we automatically enter states of concentration that resemble meditative states. For example, consider the experience of watching an extremely beautiful sunset in a state of awe and wonder. The mind becomes completely quiet and clear as you partake in the visual feast of colors and majesty. After such an experience, you indeed feel refreshed, alert, and more fully alive, just as you would after a good meditation period.

In answering the second part of your question, as to why you cannot replicate the same degree of concentration while practicing Mindfulness of Breathing, I assure you that, if you can arouse the same degree of interest in the breath, the mind will become equally focused. However, unlike the exciting computer game, the breath will not normally appear interesting to the mind. You will need to generate the interest through effort and skill. True, this is more difficult, but the rewards are well worth the effort.

CHAPTER FOUR

❦

LIFE IN THE FAST LANE
AND OTHER HINDRANCES

I F YOU HAVE BEEN PRACTICING THE MEDITATIONS
suggested in the first few chapters, you've probably
encountered some difficulties. The intention of this chapter is to help clarify the nature of the most common obstacles met by new meditators and to make some suggestions for how to deal with them. To progress on the Meditative Path, it is essential that we recognize the various hindrances that can crop up and use appropriate means to overcome them.

LIFE IN THE FAST LANE

The most obvious obstacle to achieving a peaceful and concentrated state of mind in meditation is today's frenetic lifestyle. Too many of us live in the fast lane, rushing ever more frantically to do an increasing number of things in what seems to be a decreasing amount of time. Some of this rushing is out of necessity, but a great deal of it is by choice.

The amount of effort and time needed to procure the basic requirements for living has decreased considerably with the industrial and technological developments of the last century. Despite this, people today often work longer hours and under greater pressure than ever before, not to meet their needs, but to gratify the desire for having more of everything. It is little wonder that stress is such a common affliction in our society and that there is so much interest in stress-relieving therapies and practices such as meditation.

Thus, the first obstacle to practicing meditation is not having enough free time. Unless we can find the time to practice on a regular basis, it will be virtually impossible to make much headway. Training the mind is a difficult process requiring a considerable amount of patient effort, especially at the beginning. As we develop skill in the practice, meditation does become less difficult, eventually becoming a refuge for the mind. We can only reach this goal through regular practice. Therefore, it is crucial to simplify life just enough to have a little time for meditation each day.

An athlete who kept to a regular daily training schedule was asked how he managed to motivate himself each day. He replied, "When you get up in the morning, you don't think, 'Am I going to eat today?' It is a question of when, not if! My attitude toward training is the same as toward eating." Indeed, if we really see the value of something, we make time for it.

Having made the time for practicing meditation, we will most likely encounter a second obstacle resulting from our busy lifestyle. I like to think of this hindrance as the residual fallout from sensory overload. When we sit down to meditate, we are confronted with an internal jungle of thoughts, memories, plans, hopes, and regrets. The mind is extremely busy, which should come as no surprise considering how we are living our lives.

What is a normal day for most Americans? From the moment we wake up, the mind is busy receiving and processing a phenomenal amount of information supplied by radio, television, newspapers, and the Internet. Even before finishing breakfast, we know everything about the weather, sports, financial markets, and current events from all around the world. Then there are countless activities during the day, such as driving, working, meetings, electronic mail, telephone calls, and so on. The evenings rarely provide respite because of family activities, social engagements and, on nights when there's nothing else to do, more television. Compare your typical day with a day in the life of a farmer a hundred years ago, and you begin

to appreciate both why you feel the need to learn meditation
and also why it is so difficult for you to achieve the peace you
thirst for in meditation practice.

Not many of us are interested in radically changing our
lifestyles. Few of us would want to live like a nineteenth-centu-
ry farmer, let alone become a solitary yogi living in a cave.
However, we may want to consider ways we might simplify our
lives just a little, particularly around meditation time, because
doing so makes it easier to establish awareness and concentrate
the mind. Of course, this is something for each of us to decide,
but it is important to recognize that the choices we make
regarding our lifestyle do affect our meditation practice.

THE FIVE HINDRANCES

Another group of common hindrances involve specific
mental tendencies, or habits of the mind, that create obstacles
to the development of concentration. Although we could make
a very long list of such tendencies, it will be more practical to
limit our list to five main hindrances: craving, aversion, agitation, dullness, and doubt. These hindrances act to disturb the
mind. The presence of any one of them prevents us from
achieving concentration and peace.

Craving

Craving is the thirst for experience, particularly pleasurable sensory experience. It is closely related to the most basic instinctual tendencies of all living creatures, the desire for self-preservation and self-gratification. To attempt a thorough analysis of the nature of craving, or to try and answer the question of whether it is possible for us to be completely free of craving, is beyond the scope of this book. For our purposes, it will suffice to recognize that craving is something that stirs up the mind. The tendency to want this or that, or always to want something other than what we have, makes it very difficult for the mind to abide with one object for any length of time. For this reason, craving is a serious obstacle to achieving concentration and peace.

Unfortunately, our consumer-oriented society is very much driven by the power of craving. Every advertisement, store window, and restaurant menu we see reinforces this tendency in us. Much money, time, and human ingenuity is invested in convincing us that, in order to be happy, we need more of everything. The seductions of commercialism strengthen our basic instinct for self-gratification—even exaggerate it out of proportion. No wonder our minds find it so difficult to stop chasing after things and simply rest!

How are we to deal with this habitual chasing? If we see the futility in allowing ourselves to be manipulated, or the harm in being a slave to things and experiences, we may be motivated to try to free ourselves from the grip of craving just a little, at least during the meditation period. So let us look at craving more closely.

Craving is like a black hole, for it is never satiated. How much we have, where we go, and what we experience or achieve are of no ultimate consequence, because craving will always want more. By its very nature, craving cannot be satisfied. It never knows enough!

The second insidious characteristic of craving is that it is never faithful to its object; it always wants something else. The paradox is, as Oscar Wilde put it, "There are only two misfortunes in life: getting what we want and not getting what we want!" Either way, the mind still wants whatever it does not have.

Because the tendency toward craving is so strong in the mind, we hardly ever experience the quality of contentment discussed in the last chapter. Even the wealthy are like paupers, for they, too, feel a constant need to have more. Contrast this state of affairs with the view of a simple village man in Thailand who was a devout disciple of my teacher Ajahn Chah. He would often say, "I have no money, but I am not poor!" Through his practice of meditation, this man had realized a degree of peace and contentment that no amount of money can buy. Money may buy us pleasure, but it cannot buy us contentment. That must come from within.

So what are we to do? The task of trying to free ourselves from craving is certainly daunting. However, if we begin by trying to eliminate craving for just the period of time we spend in meditation, then the idea may not seem so overwhelming. Is it possible for us to free ourselves from craving for just twenty minutes? Surely our lives will not fall apart if we stop chasing after things for such a brief time.

If during meditation you observe the mind wandering away from the breath, being led towards something else by craving, try to say, "No, not now." Practice renunciation for just this short period, and your craving may relax a bit so that you can learn to be content with one breath at a time.

By practicing in this way, the mind gradually abandons its habit of continually wanting something else and begins to rest. Once we experience the happiness of peace and contentment, the power of craving diminishes. We then appreciate the wisdom in the saying of a great master, "There is nothing more precious than to be one who has nothing further to seek."

Aversion

If we have craving for certain things, it is to be expected that we will feel aversion toward the opposite things. Craving and aversion are like the two sides of a coin; one implies the existence of the other. While craving is the tendency to chase after pleasurable and gratifying experiences, aversion is the habit of striking out at, or trying to get rid of, the things we find unpleasant, offensive, or threatening. Nothing destroys peace of mind more quickly than thoughts of aversion.

Thoughts of aversion may be directed towards other people, towards inanimate objects, or even towards ourselves. Anything that interferes with "what I want, how I want it, and when I want it" can become the object of this negative mental reaction. Of course, life rarely obliges by giving us what we want, how we want it, and when we want it, so we find ourselves experiencing these negative thoughts quite often. Being in a negative state of mind is unpleasant at any time, but if it arises during meditation, it makes practicing Mindfulness of Breathing all but impossible.

Chapter 10 is devoted to an in-depth study of the nature of aversion and explores different approaches to reducing the power of this tendency. However, at this stage, it is sufficient that we recognize the disruptive effects of aversion and make a conscious choice not to dwell on such thoughts during meditation. Our response should be like seeing a blazing fire and choosing to move away from the heat. Rather than reacting with fear and distress, we calmly find a way of making ourselves comfortable so that the mind remains balanced and composed.

Depending upon the situation, when confronted with an unpleasant or disturbing experience, we can respond in one of three ways:

- Remove the cause of the disturbing experience.
- Ignore the experience by paying attention to something else.
- Give the experience full attention and peacefully coexist with it without any negative reaction.

To illustrate these three responses, suppose that while meditating, you are bothered by noise coming through an open door. The first option is simply to close the door, thereby removing the cause of the disturbance. If that option is not available, then you can try ignoring the noise by remaining attentive to the breathing. Of course, that is easier said than done, and you may find it very difficult to pay attention to the breath when there is a lot of noise. However, for the more experienced practitioner, it is usually possible.

The third option is to stop trying to concentrate on the breathing and turn your full attention to the "world of sounds,"

silently listening and peacefully coexisting with the noise without reacting to it. What you are doing if you choose this
approach is changing the primary object of attention from the
breath and focusing your meditation on sounds. This valid and
useful meditation practice is explained more fully in Chapter 8.

Using any one of these approaches to deal with the cause
of aversion will help you remain composed. It is important to
recognize that the worst thing you can do is to continue to sit
as though meditating, while your mind is dwelling on negative
thoughts of aversion, resentment, or anger. Doing so is like
walking into the raging fire and expecting to find coolness
there. Your mind will only experience turmoil.

Agitation

When the mind is overly stimulated, it often enters a state
of agitation and restlessness, jumping from one thing to another very quickly. In its more extreme forms, agitation makes it
difficult to sit physically still, let alone achieve any degree of
mental composure in meditation.

It has already been noted that a busy lifestyle can lead to an
overactive mind. Stimulants such as coffee, tea, cola drinks, and
chocolate can exacerbate problems with restlessness. If you are
sensitive to such stimulants and tend to have a busy mind, it
may be wise to avoid these substances prior to meditation.

Trying to meditate when the mind is overactive and restless can be a very unpleasant and frustrating experience. It requires a great deal of patience as well as the application of appropriate skillful means to quiet down a restless mind sufficiently for meditation. My teacher Ajahn Chah told me that when he started practicing as a young monk, he would often experience restlessness during meditation. Determined to overcome the hindrance and not being timid by nature, he decided to fight fire with fire.

Northeastern Thailand where we lived is hot and humid for most of the year. Forest monks usually dwell in simple, single-room huts with galvanized iron roofs. During the midday heat, these huts can feel like ovens, and so, most monks seek out cooler places for meditation. However, whenever he had trouble with restlessness, my teacher told me, he would lock himself in his hut, close all the windows, put on his heavy robes, and sit cross-legged on the floor meditating until the restlessness subsided. Though his body was soaked in sweat, this patient endurance trained his mind to overcome the hindrance of restlessness.

My teacher's approach may seem rather extreme, and I am not suggesting that you emulate his method. I relate this story only to illustrate that even the most accomplished meditators have had to work to overcome the mundane hindrances that plague the rest of us. So, if you feel restless during meditation, try not to give in too easily. Be patient and experiment with the following remedies.

If the restlessness is accompanied by feelings of tension, encourage yourself to calm down and let go of everything. Direct your attention to the various parts of the body, as you learned in Chapter 1, gently relaxing the muscles and releasing all tension. As the body relaxes and the mind slows down, the restless energy will gradually dissipate. Even if this release of tension is all that you can achieve during the meditation period, it will have been a valuable experience.

However, if the mind is simply overactive and flighty, I usually recommend counting the breath in a way that requires more careful attention. Rather than just counting from "one . . . one" to "ten . . . ten" on each in breath and out breath as described in Chapter 2, you count the breath in cycles of different lengths. Thus, you begin by counting from "one . . . one" to "five . . . five" on the first round. On the next round, you count from "one . . . one" to "six . . . six," and then, on subsequent rounds, from "one . . . one" to "seven . . . seven" and so on until you reach "one . . . one" to "ten . . . ten." Counting in this way requires a great deal of attention and helps to ground a flighty mind.

Dullness and Sleepiness

While restlessness is associated with too much mental energy, it is also possible to have the opposite experience, that of having too little energy. When the mind is lethargic, we may sink into a dull state during meditation, or even drift into sleep. In this state, the attention is rather fuzzy, the head begins to droop toward the chest and the back to slump. Though we may find this state of relaxation quite pleasant and restful, it is definitely an obstacle to achieving the clarity and concentration for which we are striving. In order to make progress, we must recognize when dullness and sleepiness are upon us and take steps to overcome these obstacles.

Why does the mind sink into dullness? Quite often, it is because we are worn out from the activity associated with our fast-paced lives. After being on overdrive for so long, the mind runs out of steam and simply collapses into dullness whenever we stop moving for a few minutes. In fact, many people only know these two extremes—agitation and sleepiness—and simply alternate between the two. Either the mind is in overdrive, or it sinks into dullness, in neither case achieving that wakeful state of rest that is the goal of meditation.

Even when we are not really tired, the mind may sink into dullness during meditation simply because we are not accustomed to remaining awake and alert while withdrawing into a state of rest. What is happening in this case is that the mind is unable to generate energy from within itself without stimulation from some sensory or intellectual activity. In meditation, the intention is to empower the mind so it can remain vibrantly awake while being quiet, still, and peaceful.

The process of meditation is, in some ways, similar to the general path the mind follows when falling asleep. We begin by closing our eyes, calming down, relaxing, and letting go of all the business that usually preoccupies the mind. However, we reach a junction during this process at which there are two possible paths for the mind to follow. If awareness is weak, the mind takes the path that inclines towards dullness and sleep. It reacts in this way out of habit, if for no other reason. In this state, the mind has little or no awareness, and we have no opportunity to cultivate concentration or understanding. However, if we make a concerted effort to remain awake, alert, and mindful, the mind can take the path leading to a clear meditative state of heightened awareness. We are then able to achieve deep concentration and develop wisdom.

In order to guide the mind towards this state of restful clarity, we must be wary and cultivate awareness of any tendency to sink into dullness during meditation. Dullness or sleepiness can often overtake us when we least expect it. If the meditation period seems to pass very quickly, and you cannot recall much of what you experienced, it is quite possible that the mind drifted into dullness without your knowledge. It is important that you not allow this pattern to become a habit in your meditation practice. An easy and effective way to test your mind's clarity during meditation is to count the breath. If you repeatedly drift into a dreamlike state before successfully reaching the count of ten, you may be experiencing dullness.

What can you do when confronted with this hindrance? If you are practicing meditation for only twenty minutes a day, you do not want to spend those precious minutes fighting sleepiness. Therefore, it is best to choose a time for meditation when you are not too tired. The following techniques can also help you address this hindrance:

- Meditate in a place with some light and fresh air.
- Avoid making yourself overly comfortable or warm.
- Try to establish a good posture, keeping the back erect and the head up.
- If practicing Mindfulness of Breathing, try to sharpen the precision of your counting so that you can reach the count of ten.
- If the mind continually drifts into dullness while practicing Mindfulness of Breathing, stop trying to concentrate

on the breath and direct your full attention to the posture. Try to arouse energy in the body so that the posture remains erect, balanced, and still. Because the body is a more tangible object of attention than the breath, the mind will find it easier to focus on it. Furthermore, any tendency of the mind to sink into dullness will be readily apparent, because the posture will not remain erect if the mind is not alert. It is possible that, after practicing in this way for some time, the feeling of dullness will pass, and you can return to Mindfulness of Breathing.

• If you experience dullness in meditation quite often, try meditating with your eyes partly open.

Doubt

The last of the five hindrances that prevents us from making progress in meditation is obsessive doubt. Doubt manifests as nagging questions such as: "Is this the best method for me to use? Am I meditating the right way? How do I proceed from here? What does this mean? Should I just give up?" When the mind is stirred up by such questions, we cannot apply ourselves effectively to the task of meditation. In fact, too much doubt prevents us from applying ourselves fully to any undertaking, including work and study.

The doubting mind is closely associated with other negative tendencies such as greed, fear, and laziness. A desire to have the best of everything inevitably casts the shadow of doubt over anything we seek, because we can't be sure that what we obtain will be the best. Fear of failure or of making a mistake also stirs up doubt and hesitation and prevents us from applying ourselves with confidence. Of course, the lazy mind always wants to be certain of getting the maximum return on the minimum investment of time and energy. This type of mind can rarely make a commitment because it is constantly on the lookout for a better deal.

Such doubting tendencies can lead us around and around in endless circles, toward no meaningful end. My teacher emphasized the dangers of doubt with the following story:

A farmer needed water for his crops. He asked a neighbor where he got his water. The neighbor explained that he had dug a well that supplied his needs year round. On hearing this, the farmer decided to dig a well himself. After choosing a likely spot and digging down four or five feet, the farmer started to think that he had not chosen the right place to dig. Abandoning that hole, he started to dig in a new place. He dug down five or six feet without striking water and decided that this, too, was an unsuitable spot and so started again. After many such attempts, the farmer gave up, convinced that there was no water to be found. In fact, the water was right there under his feet, but the farmer had not dug deep enough in any one spot to reach it. In this way, doubt can frustrate all our efforts.

Of course, it is good to have an inquiring mind that is open and receptive to new knowledge and information. When approaching something new, such as meditation, we naturally have many questions that need to be answered. I hope that the information in this book addresses many of these, though the student who wishes to practice a lot of meditation will find the guidance of an experienced meditation teacher very helpful.

However, asking questions or acquiring more information from external sources cannot resolve all doubts. There comes a point when you must be willing to start practicing and be prepared to learn from experience.

Learning from Experience

It should be noted that these five hindrances do not only arise during meditation but are active, everyday states of mind. If we observe carefully, we notice that one or more of these hindrances frequently afflicts the mind. Thus, these mental tendencies are not only obstacles to progress in meditation but also the cause of a great deal of inner turmoil and outer conflict in our normal lives. However, here we are primarily concerned with recognizing and dealing with these tendencies when they arise in meditation.

It is important that we do not practice meditation in a mechanical way, just repeating the mental exercise without bothering to learn from the experience. We must reflect carefully on what we experience before, during, and after each session of meditation.

Before starting the meditation period, take a few moments to consider how you are feeling and the state of your mind. What is your energy level? Are you tired or agitated? Reflecting in this way will give you some idea of which hindrance you may need to be wary of in the meditation.

During the meditation remain watchful, being aware of how the mind is behaving. This does not mean that you should make a "running commentary" on what is happening nor allow yourself to be caught up in analyzing the experience. Your intention should be simply to notice if any particular hindrance is becoming a problem so that you can deal with it accordingly.

After the meditation, it is worthwhile to contemplate what the experience was like. If you consider what you tried to do and how it worked, you will learn a good deal from each meditation period.

By practicing in this way, you can acquire the knowledge and skill to guide the mind to a state of perfect balance and poise, undisturbed by the hindrances. Of course, that goal may not be immediately achievable, but you can make gradual progress toward achieving it.

The Analogy of a Pool of Water

The teachers in ancient India often used the analogy of a pool of water to illustrate the effects of hindrances on the mind. In an unpolluted and undisturbed pool of water in the forest, the water is so clear and still that an observer can see all the way to the bottom of the pool.

However, if the water were contaminated by colored dyes, one would not be able to see anything in the water. Similarly, if the pool were heated by an underground source so that the water was bubbling and boiling, one would not be able to see the bottom of the pool clearly. One's view would also be obstructed if the surface of the water were being blown by strong winds that caused waves on the pool, or if algae or water plants covered the pool. Lastly, if the pool were stirred up so that sediment made the water murky and black, it would be impossible to see anything other than sediment floating around.

The still, clear forest pool is like the peaceful mind resting in a state of concentration. It is clear and radiant. The colored dyes represent the hindrance of craving; the heat causing the water to boil resembles aversion; the strong wind blowing the water can be compared to agitation; the algae covering the water is like dullness; and the stirred up sediment is like doubt.

Practice diligently to overcome the hindrances, and your mind can be as clear and radiant as a still forest pool.

Exercise:
Dealing with the Hindrances

Continue practicing Mindfulness of Breathing as described in the previous chapters, but now try to introduce the element of reflection as explained above. It is common for every meditator to encounter the five hindrances at one time or another, but you may observe that one or two of these obstacles occurs more frequently in your practice. Once you've identified the problem, apply some of the suggestions given in this chapter for dealing with the particular hindrances.

It is important to remember that no two meditation periods will be identical. Try to retain a "beginner's mind" that is open and ready to learn from your experiences.

Question Time

If I try to remove craving and aversion from the mind, isn't there a danger that I will be suppressing my true feelings?

It is not so much a matter of suppression but simply of claiming our right to choose which thoughts we will dwell on and what states of mind we will encourage. Of course, before we can achieve that freedom, we need to develop sufficient mastery of the mind to be able to direct our thoughts and attention as we choose.

We do not consider it detrimental to have control over our legs so that we can walk and run. Having some control and mastery of our mental activities is similar. However, mental control is of much greater value in our quest for peace and happiness. It is quite possible for someone who is physically handicapped to live a full and happy life, but it is almost impossible for a person to achieve happiness if the mind is unable to turn away from negative thoughts and feelings.

When I read about these hindrances, I can relate to all of them. I seem to have the full complement! Is there any point in my trying to meditate?

The hindrances are mental tendencies that are common to most people. However, it is important to recognize that they are not always actively disturbing the mind. This means that the hindrances are transient states that arise in the mind for a time and then pass away. They are like visitors that come and go. It is possible for us to discourage them from visiting frequently, and when they do come, to encourage them to leave quickly. Furthermore, the hindrances generally do not over-whelm us by coming all at once. They usually visit indi-vidually, making it easier for us to deal with them.

Do not be discouraged by thinking about the length or difficulty of the journey. Just continue practicing with patient effort, taking one step at a time.

Is it true that some meditators practice for years and are still not able to attain deep levels of concentration?

Yes, it is true. But this does not mean that they derive no benefits from their practice. They inevitably acquire much understanding of the mind and develop more awareness and clarity from their years of practice. This is reflected in the way they conduct their lives, relate to other people, and deal with the problems they encounter.

The benefits of meditation are real and immediate at every level of practice, and they usually accrue gradually. One teacher compared the process to walking in the fog. As you keep walking, your clothes gradually become damp without your even noticing. In the same way, the benefits of meditation may not be "earth-shattering," but they are nevertheless of great practical significance to the meditator.

During meditation, I often find myself replaying scenes from the past and thinking about how I should have done things differently. Such thoughts makes me feel quite depressed, and I usually give up trying to meditate. How can I overcome this obstacle?

Feelings of regret and remorse are common experiences when we start on the path of introspection. As we rush through life, we keep the mind very busy, and we have little opportunity for reflecting on what we are doing or how we feel about our various experiences. When we stop rushing around and sit quietly in meditation, however, the mind is no longer swamped with new information and experiences. This respite opens some "space" in the mind that allows unresolved matters to surface.

Whatever has happened in the past, whether good or bad, wise or foolish, cannot be changed. If we dwell on the past with longing or remorse, we are not in any way altering what has already happened. We are only making ourselves miserable in the present. A far better option is to acknowledge the past for what it was and use it as a learning experience so that we can make the future better.

Thus, at the start of your meditation, remind yourself that the past is gone and cannot be changed. Resolve to abide in the present by encouraging the mind to abandon concern for both the past and the future. If during meditation your mind starts dwelling with remorse on some past event, ask yourself, "Is there anything I can do to make things better?" If the answer is "yes," then determine to do it later and put the matter aside for the remainder of the meditation. If there is nothing to be done, let the matter go. Remind yourself that the present moment offers a wonderful opportunity to cultivate greater awareness and concentration that will empower you to make better choices in the future.

CHAPTER FIVE

AWARENESS LEADS THE WAY

W E ARE NOW READY TO EXPLORE SOME OF the more refined states of meditation that can be achieved through the practice of Mindfulness of Breathing. Again, I wish to stress that the best approach to meditation is to do the practice diligently without being overly concerned with your rate of progress. My teacher would often make this point by comparing the practice of meditation with the proper method of growing a plant. The way to cultivate a plant is to look after its needs by watering it regularly, fertilizing it, and protecting it from insects. The plant will then grow at its own rate. You cannot make it grow faster by pulling at it; doing so only harms the plant. Of course, if you neglect the plant, it will probably die. The same is true with your practice of meditation. Your effort should be directed at establishing a regular practice, employing a skillful approach, and taking steps to deal with the various hindrances that arise. Progress on the path to peace will then be a natural unfolding.

Sharpening Your Awareness

In the previous chapters, I covered the first two stages in the practice of Mindfulness of Breathing:

- Knowing the in and out breath
- Knowing the long and short breath

During these early stages of practice, the emphasis is on becoming more familiar with the mind and sharpening your awareness. As long as the mind remains easily distracted or busy with thoughts, it is not possible to make much headway in establishing concentration. The mind is not yet capable of sustaining focused attention, so you simply let awareness lead the way. You know that the attention will not stay with the breath for very long, so you strive to remain very watchful. If the mind is not on the breath, what is it doing? Does the mind tend to become distracted more often during an in breath or an out breath? With vigilance and patient effort, you continue to arouse interest and carefulness in your practice.

As the power of awareness increases, the quality of wakefulness becomes more constant, so that the mind no longer falls into states of forgetfulness or distraction for any length of time.

The "drips" of awareness are merging into a flowing stream of wakefulness. When this occurs, it is possible for you to put more emphasis on strengthening concentration by focusing your attention more fully and exclusively on the breath.

Focusing your attention more fully does not require a radical change in your approach to the practice; rather, you make a subtle shift in the application of effort. At first, developing awareness was your primary concern, while concentration lagged behind. Now, establishing concentration is pushed to the forefront with the support of awareness. It is as though awareness is the foundation and concentration, the house built on this base. While the foundation was still weak, it was not possible to erect a stable structure. However, now that you have established a strong foundation of awareness, you can proceed with building a stable structure of concentration.

Developing concentration involves collecting the mind so that it can focus attention fully on the breath for a long time. Concentration can be described in terms of depth and breadth. By *depth*, we mean how fully the mind can focus on the breath. By *breadth*, we refer to how long the mind can sustain that deep focus. Thus, when practicing Mindfulness of Breathing at the more advanced stages, your effort is primarily concerned with cultivating deeper and fuller concentration for longer and longer periods of time. The practice develops both depth and breadth.

MINDFULNESS OF BREATHING III

Let us now consider how to progress to the third stage of Mindfulness of Breathing.

By now you've established a good foundation of awareness by abandoning all concern for the past and future. The mind abides more fully in the present moment and is awake and clear. You have also made some progress in subduing the disruptive influence of the hindrances; thus the mind has achieved a state of balance and poise. You experience the mind settling into a quiet and peaceful state that is pleasant and vibrant.

The flow of the breath is smooth, regular, and comfortable. Though the breath is quite subtle, it remains clear to the mind. Now, you make a gentle effort to direct and encourage the mind to embrace the breath more fully, thereby experiencing it more completely. As you do so, you'll gradually arrive at the third stage in the practice of Mindfulness of Breathing called "knowing the whole breath."

Knowing the Whole Breath

In this state of mindfulness, the mind easily perceives the complete cycle of each breath. The mind is fully present at the start of each inhalation and remains attentive while the breath flows in smoothly, through to the end of that inhalation. The mind remains content, peaceful, quiet, and alert during the short pause before the breath begins to flow out and continues to be aware of the exhalation until the end. The mind is in no hurry; it is not concerned with time. It is content and happy to experience each breath from beginning to end, savoring every peaceful moment as a timeless "now." There is no internal commentary about the breath, let alone about anything else. Within that resounding silence, you begin to experience the joy of being immersed in awareness of the breath.

It is paradoxical that to achieve this sense of fulfillment, you must empty the mind of all extraneous clutter and activity and embrace a single, simple object. Referring to the example of someone watching a passing train, at this stage the observer is enthralled by the passage of the train. Not only does he know the direction of the train and its length, but he is attentive to every car of the train, from beginning to end, fully enjoying the experience. What has happened, in fact, is that the observer has aroused a love for trains!

JOY IN MEDITATION

The process of deepening your meditation is not at all a sterile or cold experience of "just concentrating." As the mind achieves more refined levels of concentration, you not only experience a sense of profound peace, but also feelings of happiness, joy, even rapture. When you reach these stages, meditation is no longer an effort or a struggle; it is a happy respite for the mind.

The teachers of old used a metaphor to illustrate this point as well: Imagine that a man on a journey had been walking for a long time in the desert under the relentless heat of the sun. That tired, hot, and thirsty man reaches an oasis where a great tree casts a large area of cool shade next to a pool of fresh, clear water. Think of the contentment and joy the man feels while resting in the shade of the tree after quenching his thirst and washing his body in the pool.

Your experience on the path of mental cultivation is similar to that of the traveler. The mental discomfort and difficulty you experienced while the mind was being disturbed by the hindrances is similar to the physical torment of the traveler walking in the desert. However, once you reach the levels of concentration in which hindrances are no longer disturbing the mind, you experience even more profound happiness and joy than that enjoyed by the traveler resting in the cool shade.

"Bumps" on the Path to Deep Concentration

As the mind approaches deeper levels of concentration, you

may encounter two reactions that temporarily block the mind from continuing on the path. The two reactions are fear and excitement. Each can disrupt progress by preventing the mind from fully embracing the meditation object.

The fear you may experience has two aspects. One is the fear of losing your identity and sense of control; the other is a natural fear of facing the unknown. Both fears must be overcome; otherwise they will hold you back from entering deep concentration.

We derive a sense of self by identifying with our thoughts, memories, and emotions. Similarly, we feel in control when we can rationalize and analyze everything that happens with a running internal commentary. Looked at more closely, both our sense of self and our feeling of control are illusions, but we cling to these illusions because they help us feel safe. In order for the mind to enter into a deep level of concentration, we must let go of all thoughts of "what I am," as well as our usual running commentary on the experience. In other words, we must step beyond the safety of "I think therefore I am" and "I can describe and explain; therefore I am in control." Having lived so long within the confines of these illusions, we experience a natural fear of stepping out into a state of complete silence, beyond any sense of personal identity or discursive thought, where the breath can be experienced fully with simple awareness.

You cannot force the mind to abandon its illusions. However, it is possible to arouse in yourself the courage to lay down the burden of always being this or that type of person and the constant need to explain and analyze everything, at least during the period of meditation. When you encourage yourself to move in this direction, you step beyond yourself into a state of peace and silence, in which the mind experiences the joy of "simply being." It requires a degree of confidence and courage to take this step, because you are entering unknown territory. However, beyond the fear, you may discover an inner refuge, a state of being free of superficial thinking and compulsive analyzing.

Excitement can also disrupt the mind's ability to enter states of deep concentration. It is normal to become excited when you first encounter something new and wonderful. When the mind immerses itself in the breath and begins to experience the peace and joy of simple and focused awareness, it often becomes excited. Unfortunately, a mental reaction of "Wow, this is great!" effectively destroys the peaceful state that prompted the reaction in the first place. However, with more experience, you learn to avoid excess excitement so that the mind can enter and abide in deeper levels of meditation.

MINDFULNESS OF BREATHING IV

By now, you appreciate that progress in the practice of Mindfulness of Breathing involves gradually letting go of all unnecessary mental and physical activities so that the mind can move into increasingly refined and peaceful states. If you are diligent and skillful, this process leads to the advanced stage of Mindfulness of Breathing called "calming the mental and physical activities."

Calming the Mental and Physical Activities

There is nothing new or mysterious about this stage of the practice. It is, in fact, what you have been doing all along, since the early stages of meditation. However, at this stage, calming the mind and body has a more specific meaning.

Having progressed through the previous three stages of Mindfulness of Breathing, the mind is already quiet, peaceful, and calm. The breath has become subtle, and the body is completely at ease. Therefore, the process of "calming" that characterizes this fourth stage must refer to even greater levels of refinement.

Of course, you may be more than happy to achieve through your meditation practice the states of peace and joy already described. Yet, no overview of the Meditative Path would be

complete without at least a mention of the more rarefied states
of concentration attainable by the most gifted and earnest practitioners. Who knows? Perhaps you are among that number.
Here is how these states have been described by a present-day
meditation master, Venerable Ajahn Brahmavamso:

> You will find that progress happens effortlessly at this
> stage of the meditation. You just have to get out of the
> way, let go, and watch it all happen. The mind will auto-
> matically incline, if you only let it, towards this very sim-
> ple, peaceful, and delicious unity of being alone with one
> thing, just being with the breath in each and every
> moment. This is the unity of mind, the unity in the
> moment, the unity in stillness.
>
> The fourth stage is what I call the "springboard" of
> meditation, because from here one can dive into the
> blissful states. When you simply maintain this unity of
> consciousness by not interfering, the breath will begin to
> disappear. The breath appears to fade away as the mind
> focuses instead on what is at the center of the experience
> of breath, which is awesome peace, freedom, and bliss.
>
> At this stage, I use the term "the beautiful breath."
> Here the mind recognizes that this peaceful breath is
> extraordinarily beautiful. You are aware of this beautiful

breath continuously, moment after moment, with no break in the chain of experience. You are aware only of the beautiful breath, without effort, and for a very long time. . . .

The mind does not need to be forced. It stays with the beautiful breath by itself. "You" don't do anything. If you try to do something at this stage, you disturb the whole process, the beauty is lost and, like landing on a snake's head in the game of Snakes and Ladders, you go back many squares. From this stage of meditation on, the "doer" has to disappear, with just the "knower" passively observing.

A helpful trick to achieve this stage is to break the inner silence just once and gently think to yourself: "Calm." That's all. At this stage of the meditation, the mind is usually so sensitive that just a little nudge like this causes the mind to follow the instruction obediently. The breath calms down, and the beautiful breath emerges.

When you are passively observing just the beautiful breath in the moment, the perception of in breath or out breath, or of beginning or middle or end of a breath, should all be allowed to disappear. All that is known is this experience of the beautiful breath happening now. The mind is not concerned with what part of the breath cycle this breath is in, nor on what part of the body it is occurring. Here we are simplifying the object of meditation, the experience of breath in the moment, stripping away all unnecessary details, moving beyond the duality of in and out, and just being aware of a beautiful breath that appears smooth and continuous, hardly changing at all.

Do absolutely nothing and see how smooth and beautiful and timeless the breath can appear. See how calm you can allow it to be. Take time to savor the sweetness of the beautiful breath, ever calmer, ever sweeter.

Now the breath will disappear, not when "you" want it to, but when there is enough calm, leaving only "the beautiful." An analogy from English literature might help. In Lewis Carroll's *Alice in Wonderland*, Alice and the White Queen see a vision of a smiling Cheshire Cat appear in the sky. As they watch, first the cat's tail disappears, then its paws, followed by the rest of its legs. Soon the Cheshire Cat's torso completely vanishes, leaving only the cat's head, still with a smile. Then the head starts to fade into nothing, from the ears and whiskers inwards, and soon the smiling cat's head has completely disappeared—except for the smile that still remains in the sky! This is a smile without any lips to do the smiling, but a visible smile nevertheless.

This description is an accurate analogy for the process of letting go happening at this point in meditation. The cat with a smile on her face stands for the beautiful breath. The cat disappearing represents the breath disappearing, and the disembodied smile still visible in the sky stands for the pure mental object "beauty" clearly visible in the mind.

Now you let the breath disappear, and all that is left is "the beautiful." Disembodied beauty becomes the sole object of the mind. The mind is now taking its own object. You are now not aware at all of breath, body, thought, sound, or the world outside. All that you are aware of is beauty, peace, bliss, light, or whatever your perception will later call it. You are experiencing only beauty, with nothing being beautiful, continuously, effortlessly. You have long ago let go of chatter, let go of descriptions and assessments. Here, the mind is so still that you cannot say anything.

You are experiencing the first flowering of bliss in the mind. That bliss will develop, grow, become very firm and strong. Thus you enter into those states of meditation called *jhana* (absorption).

COMING BACK TO EARTH

You may consider the foregoing to be a tour through a well-established and beautifully kept garden. However, it is not yet your garden. Therefore, you must come back home and work with whatever garden you have today. More than likely, your garden needs further cultivation before it can be as beautiful as the one we just visited.

When you read descriptions of refined states of meditation, you may be affected in one of two ways. On the positive side, you may feel inspired by the wonderful possibilities that lie ahead and motivated to continue practicing with renewed enthusiasm. Unfortunately, you may also feel discouraged by the vast disparity between the reality of your experience and the description of ideal states. You may even consider abandoning the training because it seems like a hopeless endeavor. Doing so would be a great loss of your potential for inner peace and joy. Therefore, it is best to avoid all comparisons and just to continue working at your own pace. The fact that you may never run an Olympic Marathon should not discourage you from walking or jogging on a regular basis.

Tasting the Honey

I have attempted to present a comprehensive description of the practice of Mindfulness of Breathing while avoiding unnecessary terminology or complexity.

Progress in the practice has been explained in terms of four stages of development:

- Knowing the in and out breath
- Knowing the long and short breath
- Knowing the whole breath
- Calming the mental and physical activities

Taken as a whole, the practice is a gradual process of sharpening awareness and strengthening concentration by using the natural breath as the primary object of attention.

A book of meditation instructions can suggest various helpful guidelines for this process and point out some common obstacles. However, you will never know the taste of honey by reading descriptions of how wonderful it is or by analyzing its chemical composition. Only by actually tasting the honey will you know its sweetness. Similarly, only by practicing meditation yourself can you realize its fruits.

Continue to practice Mindfulness of Breathing on a regular basis. If possible, gradually increase the length of your meditation period to thirty minutes. Try to be resourceful, patient, and skillful in your endeavor and to learn from every meditation experience. Eventually, that which seems so distant will be right in front of you: awareness, concentration, serenity, and even bliss.

QUESTION TIME

I have seen photographs that appear to show meditators levitating above the ground. Are these trick photographs, or can people really do that sort of thing?

It may be true that a picture is worth a thousand words, but it does not always accurately represent reality. Although I have had the good fortune to meet many wonderful meditation masters and to study under a few for a long time, I have never witnessed any of them levitate or fly. I have seen television programs showing people meditating on the floor in a cross-legged position who spontaneously and repeatedly bounce up and down. However, this activity should not be called levitation or flying.

Developing the ability to generate the eruptive burst of energy that causes the body to bounce up into the air is not overly difficult. Nor does it require mastery of deep concentration. As mentioned in this chapter, when the mind begins to embrace the meditation object fully, the meditator experiences joy and rapture. Rapture can manifest in different ways, including the production of various sensations in the body. At this stage of concentration, the posture automatically becomes very erect because the body is full of energy. It is not uncommon for a meditator to experience this energy sweep through the body in waves that feel pleasantly exhilarating.

I view this exhilaration as a form of excitement in the mind. If it is not dealt with correctly, it can obstruct more refined and peaceful states of concentration. The wise teachers with whom I've studied advise practitioners experiencing this form of rapture to develop more calmness and serenity rather than pursue feelings of exhilaration. With deepening concentration, the manifestation of rapture subsides, and the mind experiences more refined feelings of joy and happiness.

Although bouncing up and down during meditation may make for an impressive spectacle, it is not very good for either the mind or the body. The exhilarated mind is not really peaceful, nor is it resting in a state of true serenity; it remains on edge with a type of excitement. The body is certainly not calm, because the erratic bursts of energy keep it in a state of unnecessary stimulation. To suggest that this phenomenon is the goal of meditation is at least misguided, if not harmful, in my judgment.

I have been told that the light one perceives in the mind during deep meditation is a manifestation of God. Do you agree with this view?

When the mind attains deep levels of concentration, it is common to perceive light in the mind. The manifestation of this light is dependent upon being able to reach a particular level of concentration. Regardless of the method of meditation, or of your religious beliefs, once the mind withdraws fully so that you are silent and no longer aware of the external sensory world, the original object of meditation disappears and is replaced by a purely mental image.

Of course, while in such a deep, silent, and peaceful state, there will be no thoughts or words in the mind saying, "This is beautiful light. It is white. It is blue. It is God manifesting." Only after emerging from a pro-

found meditative state will you use such words or concepts to try to describe the experience. Obviously, the
interpretation and the description you give will be
influenced by your beliefs, conditioning, and understanding. However, it is best to avoid too much label-
ing and interpretation, because all words and concepts
are in the realm of thinking about that meditation state,
while the actual experience is, in fact, beyond thought.
One of the beauties of a profound experience of meditation is that it can awaken you to the limitations of all
thoughts, concepts, and words.

For myself, I do not agree with the interpretation that
the light one sees during meditation is a manifestation
of God. I prefer to say that the perception of light in
deep meditation is a manifestation of a pure and refined
state of mind.

*In my reading, I have come across references to "insight meditation." Does this
term refer to a different type of meditation?*

"Insight meditation" has a variety of meanings depending upon who is using the words. Personally, I use the
term "insight meditation" to refer to two different, but
not unrelated, processes in meditation. First, I use the
words in the sense of "insight arising from the practice

of meditation." On the path of inner exploration, you'll inevitably discover some new things. Because the mind becomes more awake and focused in meditation, it will naturally see more clearly and deeply into the nature of thoughts, feelings, and emotions. The insights that result may range in intensity from the superficial to the most profound, but they all involve a realization in which something previously hidden or obscured suddenly becomes fully clear to the mind.

The second way I use the term "insight meditation" is in the sense of "directing the meditative mind to promote insight." By this I mean that the meditator applies awareness and attention to investigating a particular experience carefully and systematically in order to comprehend it more fully. Again, the investigation can be developed to varying degrees of refinement, which result in realizations of different intensities. In later chapters, I discuss ways to use meditation to gain insight into the nature of certain emotions and habitual tendencies.

The distinction between these two processes is significant, although subtle. In the first case, you are primarily concerned with developing awareness and concentration by practicing a meditation method such as

Mindfulness of Breathing. Insights arise spontaneously as a by-product of your practice. In the second approach, you take a more active role and apply the awareness and concentration already developed in meditation to investigating a particular phenomenon or personal issue.

Both processes require awareness and concentration. Until the mind becomes sufficiently clear and focused, no significant insight can arise, and no careful and systematic investigation can be effectively undertaken. Therefore, it is said that insight is the fruit, while awareness and concentration provide the means.

The arising of insight will naturally affect a change in your view of the world and often a corresponding change in your life. Generally speaking, as the ephemeral nature of all experience and the interrelatedness of all things become clear to the mind, you will naturally be more compassionate and less obsessive. Increasingly, peace and harmony for yourself and for all beings becomes your goal.

CHAPTER SIX

⚜

THE WALKING PATH

T HE TYPE OF MEDITATION WE HAVE BEEN
discussing up to now, Mindfulness of Breathing, is best
practiced in a sitting posture, with the meditator
remaining quite still and keeping the eyes closed. However, it is
also possible to practice meditation in other positions, including
standing and walking. This chapter explores in some detail the
practice of Walking Meditation.

In Walking Meditation, the primary object of attention, the
anchor for the mind, is not the breath, but rather the process of
walking itself. In other words, as we practice, we pay close
attention to the physical act of walking, the way we take one
step after another. However, though the posture and the object
of attention have changed, the overall goal of the meditation
remains the same. We are still pursuing a path of mental culti-

vation through which we are trying to develop greater awareness, concentration, and serenity.

Adding Walking Meditation to your practice may be compared to introducing a different type of physical exercise into your fitness training program. Having exercised on a treadmill for a while, you may want to try swimming for a change. But your aim is still the same; you want to be fit and healthy.

Benefits of Walking Meditation

Although Walking Meditation is not as well known or as widely practiced as sitting meditation, it is nevertheless a valuable method of mental training with some unique characteristics that can strengthen and broaden your practice.

In Mindfulness of Breathing, the object of attention is rather subtle; in Walking Meditation the object is far more obvious and tangible. Focusing on a more obvious object of attention can help you avoid two extremes that meditators sometimes experience while practicing Mindfulness of Breathing. First, you are less likely to fall into a state of dullness or sleepiness because you are actually walking with your eyes open. In fact, Walking Meditation is often recommended for practitioners who are having a problem with the hindrance of dullness.

Furthermore, as Walking Meditation is not usually practiced with the same intensity of concentration as Mindfulness of
Breathing, there is less chance that you will create tension by
using excessive force in an effort to focus the mind. Walking is
generally a pleasant and relaxing experience for both the mind
and body and is, therefore, an excellent form of meditation for
relieving stress.

Another advantage of Walking Meditation is of more relevance to practitioners doing a lot of meditation. In a meditation
retreat, participants often practice for many hours each day.
Sitting for long periods inevitably causes some physical discomfort. Alternating between sessions of sitting and walking
meditation relieves this discomfort in a pleasant way and makes
it possible for participants to maintain a continuity of practice
over a long time.

You may also find that on occasions such as after a full meal
or when you are feeling tired, Walking Meditation can be easier to practice and more effective than Mindfulness of Breathing.

Finally, Walking Meditation greatly facilitates the transition
from formal meditation to Meditation in Action. The next
chapter discusses this much broader approach to the process of
mental cultivation, in which ordinary daily activities become
part of meditation practice. Walking Meditation can be a bridge
between formal sitting practice and some of the more informal

aspects of meditation. If you can learn to establish awareness and focus while moving physically with the eyes open, you will find it easier to arouse those same qualities during other daily activities, thereby helping you transform ordinary life into a continuous practice of meditation.

When I discuss the benefits of Walking Meditation, I often recall an inspiring event that occurred during the height of the Vietnam War. The well-known meditation master Venerable Thich Nhat Hanh, a prominent figure in the peace movement, was touring the United States giving public talks and participating in demonstrations. Obviously, people had strong feelings, and any demonstration could easily turn into a disruptive confrontation.

Fortunately, into the midst of that highly charged emotional atmosphere, Thich Nhat Hanh's presence brought the irresistible power of a truly peaceful being. I can still see in my mind the picture of this simple, Buddhist monk, at the head of a demonstration of thousands of people marching through the main street of an American city, walking slowly, silently, peacefully. With each step, it was as if time paused, and the aggressive, restless energy of the city was miraculously calmed.

On that day, Thich Nhat Hanh did not talk about peace, but the reverberating message of each slow, meditative step was heard by all. As Thich Nhat Hanh has written:

Although we walk all the time, our walking is usually more like running. When we walk like that, we print anxiety and sorrow on the Earth. We have to walk in a way that we only print peace and serenity on the Earth. We can all do this, provided that we want it very much. Any child can do it. If we can take one step like this, we can take two, three, four, and five. When we are able to take one step peacefully and happily, we are walking for the whole of humankind. Walking meditation is a wonderful practice. (*Peace in Every Step*, 28)

I very much encourage you to make Walking Meditation part of your practice, if not on a regular basis, then at least on some occasions.

THE WALKING PATH

Walking Meditation is a formal meditation technique. As such, it is best practiced on a designated path rather than by casually walking about. The path chosen for practice should be straight, level, and have a reasonably smooth surface. It is also helpful that the path be one with a beginning and an end. We practice meditation by walking between these two points, being attentive and mindful of each step. Although the length of the path is primarily determined by individual preference, I have found that a path in the range of ten to twenty yards is most useful.

Choosing a path with a beginning and an end is important because these two points provide structure for the meditation and foster sharper awareness. Each time we come to the end of the path, we are automatically reminded to check to see whether the attention is indeed with each step, or whether the mind has wandered off. In this way, we can reestablish focus more quickly and sustain more constant awareness.

The length of the path is also significant. It is important that the path not be too short, because frequent stops and turns can lead to physical discomfort and become a distraction for the mind. If the path is too long, on the other hand, we may find it difficult to sustain careful attention and awareness for its entire length, and the mind may slip away into distracted thinking more easily. I suggest that you experiment with paths of different lengths and find the one most suitable for your practice.

GENERAL INSTRUCTIONS FOR WALKING MEDITATION

The instructions for Walking Meditation are much the same as for the practice of Mindfulness of Breathing. Choose an appropriate time, and decide how long to meditate. It may be a little more difficult to find a suitable place, because more space is needed for Walking Meditation. The walking path can be either inside or outside, depending upon your preference and the area available. However, it is best that the area be quiet, so that you are not distracted by external activity or by feeling self-conscious while pacing up and down along the same path. Whenever possible, it is better to practice Walking Meditation in bare feet, but this is not essential.

Having established these conditions, stand at one end of the path. It is better to hold your hands gently together in front of or behind your body rather than allowing them to hang by the sides. The eyes remain open, gazing down along the path about two yards ahead. The intention is not to be looking at anything in particular but simply to see that you are remaining on the path and that you know when to turn around.

You should now try to center yourself by putting aside all concern for the past and the future. In order to calm the mind and establish awareness in the present, abandon any preoccupation with work, home, relationships, and all the rest. Intentionally leave all those thoughts outside and bring the attention to the body, being aware of the body standing still. The mind is standing with the body.

The meditation exercise is simply to walk at a slow, relaxed pace, taking one step at a time, being fully aware of each step, until you reach the end of the path. Begin with the right foot.

While taking that step, pay careful attention from beginning to end. Then, take a step with the left foot, being equally attentive. Continue walking in this mindful way until you reach the end of the path.

If while walking you become aware that the mind has wandered away from the step, you should clearly note the distraction and gently but firmly bring the attention back to the step. You are peacefully walking, quietly walking, enjoying taking one step at a time, with nothing else to do and nowhere to go.

It is often helpful to make a mental note of "right" . . . "left" with each corresponding step, because this noting keeps the mind more involved with the act of walking.

When you arrive at the end of the path, stop for a moment and check to see what the mind is doing. Is the mind being attentive? If necessary, reestablish awareness, centering yourself by abandoning any distraction that may have arisen. Then, turn around and walk back to the other end in a similar fashion, remaining mindful and alert.

Continue to pace up and down for the duration of the meditation period, gently making an effort to sustain awareness and focus attention on the process of walking.

WALKING AT DIFFERENT SPEEDS

Walking Meditation may be done in a number of ways that

require different degrees of concentration. While walking at a normal pace is suitable for developing awareness, very slow walking is more effective for refining concentration. Therefore, I usually practice and teach two styles of Walking Meditation.

Walking at a Normal Pace

Here, we mindfully pace up and down on the meditation path as described, walking at a normal pace or one just a little slower than normal. When walking in this way, it is best to focus attention on the general experience of the foot taking the step. Do not try to concentrate on any particular detail but simply strive to remain aware of each step. Practicing Walking Meditation in this manner is good for cultivating awareness, and it can produce a very pleasant and peaceful experience.

Slow Walking

If you wish to use Walking Meditation to develop stronger concentration, then it is preferable to walk at a much slower pace. In this case, you pay close and detailed attention to each individual step, fully experiencing the foot as it is lifted off the ground, moved through the air, and placed on the ground again. Because walking in this way requires more careful and focused attention, it can develop more profound concentration.

As in the practice of Mindfulness of Breathing, it is best to establish a good foundation of awareness before trying to concentrate the mind more fully. Once awareness is sharp and the mind has become somewhat quiet, it will be easier to focus attention more intensely on each step. You may wish to begin practicing Walking Meditation at a normal pace until the mind is calm and then experiment with the more intense form of slow walking.

Although it is not possible to achieve the same depth of concentration as in Mindfulness of Breathing, you can certainly develop very peaceful, clear, and concentrated states of mind through the practice of Walking Meditation. As with any meditation method, you will need to arouse the qualities of interest, carefulness, and contentment and to be wary of the various hindrances that can arise. As before, regular practice can help develop your skill.

A FINAL WORD

From experience, I have discovered that meditators generally have a preference for one posture rather than another in their practice of meditation. More people seem to prefer sitting meditation, because it can lead to more refined states. But I have met practitioners who favor Walking Meditation.

Whichever method you choose, remember that regardless of what posture your body is in, you are always working with your mind. Thus, whatever qualities of awareness and concentration are developed in one form of meditation should be easily transferable to another. The practices of Mindfulness of Breathing and Walking Meditation augment each other. Both flow towards peace, just as rivers flow into the ocean.

EXERCISE: WALKING MEDITATION

Using the instructions given in this chapter as your basic guidelines, practice Walking Meditation for a period of twenty minutes. You may find a corridor in your home or a pathway in the garden to be suitable for this exercise. Of course, it is very pleasant to walk in a natural setting, such as on a secluded path in a shaded forest where you can "leave the troubles of the world behind," but if such a place is not convenient, make the most of whatever path is available to you.

Give yourself time to become familiar with this form of meditation. Try to encourage the mind to slow down and relax into the walking. Walk peacefully, walk quietly, and enjoy the walk.

You may find that the mind tends to have more thoughts and to be more easily distracted during Walking Meditation than while practicing Mindfulness of Breathing. This is quite natural, because the process of walking with the eyes open is a more relaxed state that gives the mind more scope for movement. Do not be discouraged by the thoughts that may arise. Rather, regard them as an opportunity to foster sharper awareness by noticing the movements of the mind and continually guiding it back to the act of walking.

Gently teach the mind to abandon the burden and complexity of thinking, planning, remembering, and worrying about things. Feel everything drop away as your attention sinks down toward your feet and you become grounded in the act of taking a single step. Experience the simplicity, peace, and beauty of being with one step at a time, with nothing else to do and nowhere to go—peacefully walking, quietly walking, and enjoying the walk.

QUESTION TIME

Can I concentrate on the breath while doing Walking Meditation?

Some teachers encourage their students to use the breath as the primary object of attention during Walking Meditation. Some also combine the rhythm of breathing with the walking pace. Personally, I have not found either of these approaches to be really comfortable or effective, and so, I do not teach those styles of Walking Meditation. To me it feels much more natural to take the process of walking itself as the primary object of attention. However, if a particular meditation approach helps you develop better awareness and concentration, by all means use it!

I have read that in some traditions, Walking Meditation is practiced on a circular path rather than on a straight one. Is there any difference between the two approaches?

No. I believe that both approaches are valid, provided that you are comfortable with the conditions and method. I have practiced both styles of Walking Meditation and see advantages and disadvantages in each.

As I explained, walking on a straight path with a beginning and an end helps remind us to check what the mind is doing every time we reach the end of the path. While most of us may find this useful, others may experience the frequent stopping and turning as tedious and prefer to walk on a circular, continuous path. All that really matters is that we are able to establish and maintain awareness during the meditation period.

I have noticed that some meditators walk at an extremely slow pace during Walking Meditation. Doing so seems very unnatural. Why do people walk like that?

Some traditions teach a very intense form of Walking Meditation that requires paying careful attention to every detail in each step. In order to cultivate awareness of subtle details, the pace of walking must be very slow and deliberate. While this style of walking may be suitable for developing intense concentration, it often requires slowing down so much that the meditator is no longer walking in the ordinary sense of the word.

I find that walking at a more normal pace feels much more comfortable and helps us develop awareness during normal activity. I consider such awareness to be of great benefit, because it begins to broaden the scope of practice beyond a specialized technique. As will be explained in the next chapter, one of the goals of the Meditative Path is to integrate the practice of meditation into ordinary life. Ultimately, we can bring the quality of meditative awareness into every moment of life and experience the miracle of being awake.

You made reference to retreats where people meditate for many hours every day. How are meditation retreats organized, and how will I know if I am ready for such an intense type of practice?

Traditionally, meditators occasionally seek the opportunity to spend some time in private retreat. By remaining in relative solitude and being quiet, they can devote themselves more fully to the practice of introspection and mental cultivation. Often, they go to a monastery or retreat center for this purpose, because conditions there are more conducive to intense practice.

In addition to this kind of "self-retreat," many groups today organize structured retreats for large numbers of meditators under the guidance of a teacher. These retreats often take place over a period of one to ten days, or occasionally longer. They are usually held in meditation centers where participants are provided with food and accommodations so that they are not preoccupied with mundane cares. The retreats are often conducted in silence, with a daily schedule of meditation periods, instruction, interviews with the teacher, meals, and so on. The specific structure of the retreat and style of meditation depends upon the teacher and the tradition of the organizing group.

Such retreats are indeed wonderful opportunities for you to learn a lot about the mind and to establish yourself more firmly on the Meditative Path. However, retreats require an intense level of practice, and I would recommend that you first consult the teacher with regard to your level of experience and readiness for a retreat experience. You may be advised to start with a half-day or one-day retreat before venturing into a longer one. This is not to say that a new meditator should not attempt a longer retreat, or that you would not benefit from it, but you must be prepared for an experience that can be somewhat demanding. A good teacher can help you to make the appropriate decision.

CHAPTER SEVEN

⚜

MEDITATION IN ACTION

BOTH MINDFULNESS OF BREATHING AND WALKING Meditation involve a systematic training of the mind under very special conditions. In both cases, the meditator practices a specific mental exercise at a particular time in a special place in order to develop refined levels of awareness, concentration, and serenity. These and other types of what we might call "formal meditation" are the backbone of the Meditative Path. However, there is more to meditation than just these formal techniques.

As meditation is concerned with studying and training the mind, and because this very same mind is involved in every aspect of living, it should be possible to merge the practice of meditation with normal daily life. However, this merging does not happen spontaneously. It takes effort to cultivate a meditative state of mind during ordinary and routine activities. I refer to this merging of the Meditative Path with everyday life as "Meditation in Action."

Unfortunately, when meditation is taught in the West, this valuable and important aspect of the training is often ignored. Within the monastic tradition in which I trained, my teacher greatly stressed the need to practice meditation beyond the formal periods of sitting and walking. He promoted the cultivation of mindfulness throughout the day in every activity, including eating, talking, walking, and while doing all chores.

Although the training that I received was intended for monastics, I feel that the techniques of Meditation in Action are equally valid and possibly even more important for people living ordinary lives. The reason for this view is quite simple. In a monastery, practitioners are given the opportunity and are actually required to do many hours of formal meditation every day. Thus, even if they do no other practice, meditation is already a large part of the residents' daily routine.

By contrast, most of us probably manage to meditate for only thirty minutes a day on a regular basis. Because the time spent in meditation practice is so brief, it may be difficult for us to realize the full benefits of meditation unless we can find some way to engage in a more comprehensive practice. Fortunately, it is possible to broaden the scope of our practice so that it gradually includes an increasing portion of life. We do this by learning to put our meditation into action so that we live with mind-fulness throughout the day.

A Meditative State Suitable for Daily Life

Let's remind ourselves of the basic mental qualities that constitute a meditative state:

- *Awareness:* the quality of knowing where the attention is now

- *Concentration:* the ability to focus attention on one object

- *Serenity:* a mental state of peace

During formal meditation, we establish special conditions that help us develop refined levels of these three qualities. Now, how can we establish these same qualities in ordinary life? Obviously, we cannot concentrate on our breathing while we are walking, talking, driving, working, and doing all the other things that constitute a normal life. Not only would such focus be impractical; it would also be unsafe!

Living an ordinary life requires that we remain receptive to a variety of sensory information, process it accordingly, and respond in an appropriate manner. It is sometimes necessary for us to concentrate exclusively on a particular activity for a while, as when we are reading a book or balancing a checkbook. But more often, our attention needs to remain fluid, because life is a flowing process of changing experiences.

Unlike concentration that requires that we focus on a single object, awareness has the ability to flow from one thing to another. Awareness is like a light that illumines whatever occupies the mind at a particular moment. Therefore, awareness can remain continuously present while the mind is receiving and processing information during the ordinary experiences of life. While activity may be an obstacle to concentration, it is not necessarily an obstacle to awareness. It is possible to talk, walk, eat, drive, work, and do the thousand other things we do each day while remaining fully aware.

The obstacle to awareness is forgetfulness or heedlessness. When we are heedless, we forget to be fully awake in the present moment and drift into a state lacking clarity and mindfulness. If we can overcome the obstacle of forgetfulness through vigilance and wakefulness, it is possible to maintain awareness throughout the day. Awareness is the single quality that can transform ordinary activity into a practice of meditation. Put simply, Meditation in Action is the practice of developing awareness as we engage in ordinary daily activities.

The Difference Between Light and Dark

Having embarked on the journey of introspection through the practices of Mindfulness of Breathing and Walking Meditation, we can appreciate the subtle but critical difference between being aware and just being conscious in the normal sense. When there is awareness, we are fully present, awake, and sensitive to the experience of the moment and able to choose how we respond.

Whatever task we undertake is done better if we can arouse awareness, because awareness involves the mind fully in an activity. If we are listening to someone talk, awareness allows us to hear clearly and understand what the person is saying. If we are reading, awareness helps us to comprehend and be receptive to the meaning of the text. When we are walking with awareness, the mind is walking with the body rather than being lost in thought a thousand miles away. The contrast between mindful living and heedless existence is like the difference between light and dark.

Regretfully, most of us live a good portion of our lives in the dark, drifting from one moment of half-hearted attention to another of distraction. During a radio interview, an expert on the driving habits of English motorists was asked to assess what percentage of time the drivers of cars were actually concentrating on driving. His answer, which may frighten you into commuting by train, was that drivers are fully involved in the act of driving only about twenty-five percent of the time. This means that for three-quarters of the time they spend behind the wheel, drivers are operating on automatic pilot, their minds lost in one distraction or another. Though this statistic may sound like an exaggeration, if we stop and reflect on our own daily experience, we may discover that the expert was rather generous in his assessment.

How often have you listened to a speech and then realized that you missed a good portion of what was said because the mind had drifted off to something else? How many times have you reached the end of a memo or letter only to find that you remember nothing about what you just read?

Indeed, life is full of such moments. That is why we miss out on so much. We seem to "wake up" only when some extraordinarily pleasant or unpleasant experience is happening. This tendency may be why so many of us continually seek the thrill of something exciting, because only then do we feel alive. But most of life is ordinary, and if we can remain "awake" only during those few exciting moments, then we are not going to live very full or rewarding lives.

THE MIRACLE OF BEING AWAKE

How can we make the ordinary something worthy of attention? How can we transform the mundane into the miraculous? The power is within us. It is the same quality that enables us to arouse interest in the breath while practicing Mindfulness of Breathing or in the step during Walking Meditation. If we arouse enough interest to bring awareness into the moment so that the mind is fully present, we have the ability to awaken in every moment.

Awareness is the essential thread that runs through every aspect of meditation and unifies them into the Meditative Path. Without awareness, insight and mental cultivation are impossible, as are sensitivity to experiences and the ability to choose our responses. The less awareness we have, the more trapped we are in our habitual reactions to situations. Without awareness, we cannot change our pattern of behavior, even when we sincerely want to do so.

The arising of awareness shines a light that allows us to see clearly what is happening, what we are experiencing, and what we are doing. It helps to bring about a state of wakefulness and clarity in which we can claim our right to choose how we want to be in each moment. Awareness opens the door that leads to a new way of being.

As a traditional Tibetan saying puts it: "An art of living, which will enable one to utilize each activity as an aid on the Path is indispensable." The practice of Meditation in Action is just such an art of living.

CULTIVATING AWARENESS IN DAILY LIFE

In Japan, there was once an old monk who lived alone in a small meditation hermitage in the mountains. He went about his daily chores with a careful grace that reflected his inner peace and clarity. He had, however, one peculiarity. Every now and then, for no apparent reason, he called out his own name. By this simple action, it is taught, he brought himself back into the present moment, reestablishing awareness whenever he noticed that his mind had drifted into forgetfulness.

Although it is not necessary for us to adopt that monk's method of practice, this story illustrates the obstacle we face when we try to arouse awareness in daily life. Though we may sincerely aspire to be awake in every moment, doing so is difficult because of the power of habit and forgetfulness. Therefore, rather than expecting to achieve continuous awareness immediately, we begin by developing mindfulness around a small number of routine tasks. Then, as we become more skilled at maintaining awareness in the mind, we gradually incorporate more aspects of daily life into the practice of Meditation in Action.

It is important to understand that to develop awareness in daily life we do not need to go around with an empty mind. Rather, we strive to be awake and centered in the present, clearly knowing at each moment what we are doing. For instance, if you are walking down the street to the bus stop, the mind knows that the body is walking. If thoughts, plans, or memories come into the mind, the mind is aware of them. When you come to an intersection, you know it and can decide whether or not it is safe to cross.

Naturally, thoughts, plans, and memories may come up while we are engaged in an activity, but these need not be an obstacle to awareness. The obstacle of forgetfulness arises from our habitual tendency to get lost in a jungle of thoughts, one leading to another without conscious direction or purpose. If it is necessary to plan for the future, then by all means we should do so, and make the best plan possible. But we should plan for the future with awareness and clarity, rather than just by daydreaming.

Through the practice of Meditation in Action, you come to realize that a good portion of thinking is habitual. The restless mind fills with idle chatter to keep it occupied because it does not know how to relax. Unfortunately, all this clutter stifles the mind, keeping it from developing important and meaningful insights. Through awareness, we can thin out the jungle of thoughts, discarding a lot of the trivial and useless chatter so that we can experience greater clarity.

When we are practicing Meditation in Action, we still experience thinking, seeing, hearing, feeling, and other mental and physical activities, but we remain centered on whatever main activity we are involved in at that moment. When trivial thoughts come into the mind, we let them go, because there is something more important and meaningful for the mind to be involved in—the present experience. If something important comes up that needs to be thought about, and it is a suitable time to be thinking about such things, then we can, of course, think about it. When we do, this new thought becomes the present activity for the light of awareness. Like sunshine, the light of awareness shines on each thing so that it becomes clear.

SOME SUGGESTIONS FOR PRACTICING MEDITATION IN ACTION

It's a good idea to begin your practice of Meditation in Action by choosing to shine the light of awareness on four or five routine daily activities. Performing these simple tasks with awareness helps you develop a better appreciation for what the practice is trying to achieve. Here are a few suggestions for how to get started:

Brushing Your Teeth

Most of us brush our teeth twice a day, but we rarely do so with much attention. Usually, while the hand is brushing, the mind is busy thinking or daydreaming, and neither the brushing nor the thinking is done with any real interest. If negative thoughts come into the mind, we may brush in an aggressive manner using excessive force. If the mind is hyperactive and restless, the brushing will tend to be haphazard. Unfortunately, this mechanical way of brushing not only results in more trips to the dentist, but it also perpetuates and reinforces the habits of mental carelessness and heedlessness.

How can you make the act of brushing your teeth a practice of meditation? There is no need for you to brush your teeth in a stylized manner using some special technique. You need only center yourself and bring the mind into the present by thinking, "What am I doing?" Rather than just moving the brush back and forth mechanically, you encourage the mind to be fully involved in the act of brushing.

So begin by intentionally deciding that you want to transform this routine activity of brushing your teeth into a practice of meditation. For these few minutes, relax into the present moment and brush your teeth in a natural way but with awareness.

- Pick up your toothbrush . . . is it your toothbrush?
- Apply the toothpaste . . . how much toothpaste do you use?
- Begin to brush your teeth . . . which teeth do you brush first?

Continue to brush your teeth with this sort of interest, being aware of how much pressure you are applying and what area you are brushing, making sure that you actually brush all the teeth.

Of course, thoughts will come into the mind, but because there is awareness, you will notice the thinking. If what arises in the mind is just trivial chatter, let it go, and come back to brushing your teeth, keeping your mind and body together throughout the activity.

A dentist once told me that to brush the teeth properly, we should brush for about three minutes. If you brush your teeth with awareness, then not only will your teeth be cleaner, but you will have also practiced three minutes of meditation! When you practice Meditation in Action, you do not have to "make time" for meditation; rather, you discover that you have all the time you need because you live more fully in each moment.

Showering

Showering is a most pleasant and relaxing daily activity, but most of the time we do not really experience it. While the body is in the shower, the mind is busily someplace else. But not any longer! Next time you take a shower, make sure that the mind is taking a shower with the body.

Bring your attention into the present moment and notice the pleasant feeling of the water on your body. Allow the warmth of the water to soothe and relax the muscles, relieving all the built up tension. Try to keep the mind with the body as you soap up, enjoying the fragrance of the soap and the smooth feeling of it on your body. When you rinse off, let all the cares of life fall away, just like the soap that is being rinsed away. While drying the body, encourage the mind to be there, experiencing and enjoying the feel of the towel on the skin.

Whatever thoughts, memories, or plans pass through the mind, simply know them and deal with them as seems appropriate. Again, you may find that most of the mental activity is just habitual chatter. Let it go, and continue to enjoy these pleasant moments. After showering in this way, not only will you be physically cleansed and refreshed, but you will also feel mentally refreshed, centered, and clear.

Walking

Many people take up walking for health reasons, but all too often, the result is "mindless bodies" walking for exercise. Why not make better use of this activity?

In the previous chapter, I described the practice of Walking Meditation. It is also possible to develop awareness during an ordinary daily walk. Going for a pleasant stroll in the park can be an excellent opportunity for developing Meditation in Action.

To make your stroll a meditation, simply walk in your usual way, but encourage the mind to walk with the body. Relax into the present moment, allowing the mind to become quiet and to enjoy the pleasure of rhythmic movement. Your mind and body are together, peacefully walking, enjoying the walk. As a traditional saying puts it, "Tread gently in this place of peace, and peace will be with you."

If you are walking in a park with trees and flowers, notice the beauty of nature by staying fully present to what's around you in each moment. Whatever goes through the mind, just know it as mental "stuff." Is it really worth bothering about? Is it important enough to take you away from what is right here, right now? If there is something really important that you need to think about, then do so with awareness. But if what's running through the mind is just trivial, leave it behind and continue to enjoy the walk.

When the mind and body walk together in this way, not only do we benefit physically, but we realize how wonderful it is to be awake.

Washing Dishes

Most people do not like washing dishes and do so with a lot of negative thoughts and feelings that make the chore a miserable experience. Other people wash dishes in a half-hearted way, mainly daydreaming, which results in many chipped and broken dishes. One meditation teacher told me that he could assess the general quality of meditation among the students by the number of chipped cups in the kitchen!

Since we need to wash dishes, why not transform this mundane task into an opportunity for meditation? Again, center yourself, and bring the mind into the present by being aware of what you are doing now:

- Feel the temperature of the water in the sink . . . is it hot enough?
- Add detergent . . . how much are you using?
- Wash each dish . . . have you scrubbed every surface?
- Rinse each dish . . . how clean is it?

Since the mind has also been washing the dishes, the dishes get washed more carefully. When you have finished, clean the sink and enjoy the feeling of having completed a task and done it well. It is extremely gratifying to transform a sink full of messy dishes into a stack of sparkling clean dishes. But it is even more gratifying to know that, by taking this opportunity to practice Meditation in Action, you are bringing greater peace and clarity to everyday life.

Many of the chores you do around the house can be used in a similar way to practice Meditation in Action. Doing so takes no extra time and requires no special conditions. Washing the car, gardening, sweeping, vacuuming, painting, and many other activities can become part of your meditation practice. All you need to do to transform these chores into meditation is to establish and maintain awareness while doing them.

Driving

I once saw a cartoon strip that illustrates the habits of today's drivers perfectly. A man is driving a car along the highway. In each consecutive panel, the man is doing one extra thing in addition to driving. First, the man is just driving; then he is driving and listening to the radio; next he is driving, listening to the radio, and eating a sandwich. Finally, he is driving, listening to the radio, eating a sandwich, and talking on a cellular phone!

Perhaps we're not as dangerously busy as this man when we drive, but how often are we really aware of what we're doing at each moment? Next time you drive your car, try practicing Meditation in Action for a little while. Turn off the radio and relax into driving in a wakeful manner. Driving requires that you remain aware of many things in a continuously flowing way, so you need to stay in the moment. If you are driving with awareness:

- You will know your speed . . . are you within the speed limit?

- You will notice the car ahead of you . . . are you too close?

- You will keep an eye on the rearview mirror . . . what is behind you?

- If there are traffic lights coming up, you will see them . . . are they red or green?

Many thoughts will pass through the mind, but you'll continually bring your attention back to the present and drive with awareness. Even if the thoughts seem very important, this is not the time to practice awareness of thinking! It is too dangerous. When driving, it is best just to drive.

If more people practiced driving with awareness, the number of car accidents would diminish. So try gradually to broaden the scope of your practice of Meditation in Action to include time spent behind the wheel. You will find that, in addition to being safer, driving will be a much less stressful experience.

Eating

The last exercise I wish to recommend is what I call the "apple meditation."

Most of us like food, talk a lot about food, and sometimes spend a lot of money to eat in expensive restaurants. But how often are we actually present to the full experience of eating? Part of the reason we do not pay much attention to eating is because it often takes place in a social setting with conversation and other activity going on. If you are having dinner with a friend who wants to discuss something important, it certainly would not be appropriate for you to be overly interested in the taste of your food. There is a time and place for everything.

However, when you have an opportunity, try this exercise in mindfully eating. Choose an apple or some other fruit of your liking and sit down comfortably so that you can enjoy eating this apple. Begin by peeling the apple with a knife, going around carefully so that the peel comes off in one long, continuous strip. You will quickly discover that if your mind is too busy or distracted, the peel will not form one single strip. So bring awareness into the activity of peeling.

Having peeled the apple, slice it and eat one slice at a time. Feel the texture of the apple as you chew, savor the flavor, and swallow each mouthful before eating the next slice. No need for a running commentary; simply discard the unnecessary chatter and be fully present to the experience of eating this wonderful apple.

Drop by drop,
The bucket is filled.
Moment by moment,
Awareness is developed.

As explained earlier, our goal is to incorporate as much of our daily activity as possible into our practice of Meditation in Action, so that living and meditation merge into one process— a meditative life. A great Chinese master described this practice with these words:

How wonderful!
Quite miraculous!
I am fetching water!
And carrying wood!
(Timothy Freke, *Zen Wisdom*, 122)

We may never achieve such a lofty state of full awareness, but through vigilant effort we can become more centered, awake, and peaceful in the midst of daily activity.

THE RELATIONSHIP BETWEEN FORMAL AND INFORMAL MEDITATION

Formal meditation and Meditation in Action are two aspects of a single process of mental cultivation. Throughout this process we strive to develop awareness, concentration, and serenity; however, the intensity and emphasis of the practice is determined by what we are doing at the moment.

Formal meditation is an intense form of mental training under special conditions that makes it possible for us to develop strong concentration and refined awareness. In the practice of Meditation in Action, we are more concerned with establishing a general state of mindfulness with less emphasis on concentration. During both forms of practice, however, we strive to arouse awareness, because awareness is essential to every aspect of the Meditative Path.

Since awareness is common to both types of practice, whichever practice we develop automatically strengthens the other. That is to say, by practicing formal meditation, we automatically make it easier to practice Meditation in Action because we have learned to establish awareness more effectively. Similarly, developing awareness in daily life makes it much easier to achieve good concentration during formal meditation because the mind will be reasonably clear at the start of the meditation session.

A good analogy for the way these two types of practice support each other is training the body. Say that you join a health club and participate in an aerobics class. In the class, you use special exercises to strengthen the heart, lungs, and muscles. When you finish the class and go about your normal activities of walking, working, cleaning, and so on, you are still using the heart, lungs, and muscles. In fact, you are continuing to exercise those muscles, though not with the same intensity. Doing aerobics on a regular basis helps your body stay fit and strong so that you can do ordinary chores quite easily. In a reciprocal way, staying physically active in your ordinary life with housework, walking, gardening, and so on fosters a general sense of good health that makes it easy for you to enjoy the aerobics class at the health club.

Practicing formal meditation is similar to going to the health club for an intensive workout, while Meditation in Action is like keeping ourselves healthy by leading an active life. Both aspects of the Meditative Path are valuable, and each supports the other. Taking a holistic approach to the practice of meditation and cultivating all aspects of the path is, therefore, a wise decision.

QUESTION TIME

While browsing in the bookstore, I noticed a book titled Zen and the Art of Motorcycle Maintenance. *Would that be the same as Meditation in Action?*

That is a very enigmatic title and it could mean a number of things. However, if you were developing awareness around the activities involved in the regular maintenance of a motorcycle, then you would be practicing Meditation in Action. Thinking in this way, we probably could also develop "Zen and the art of cooking," "Zen and the art of ironing clothes," "Zen and the art of window washing," "Zen and the art of swimming," and so forth. Indeed, there could be many books written about this one practice—mindfulness in every action.

Do athletes and people who master a particular sport need to have the meditative kind of mental clarity and focus in order to achieve success?

I think you will find that truly accomplished people in any type of work or sport will have a highly developed ability to apply their minds exclusively to the activity in which they are involved. Of course, they will also have the intellectual or physical attributes required for that task. But all other things being reasonably equal, what usually distinguishes a great athlete from an ordinary one is that person's mental attitude and ability to be completely present, clear, and focused during the activity.

The following advice given by a Japanese master is, perhaps, appropriate for any athlete:

> Try not to focus your mind anywhere in particular, but rather let it fill all your body. Let it flow through your whole being. Then you will find you spontaneously use your hands when necessary and your legs or eyes when needed, without wasting time and energy. (Timothy Freke, *Zen Wisdom*, 77)

If we can develop awareness around every activity, does it follow that we can cultivate our meditation practice even when we're having a great time at a party with a few drinks, lots of music, and lively conversation?

I am sorry to disappoint you, but some things do not mix very well. You will find that the effects of a "few drinks" and all the distractions at a party make it almost impossible for you to retain much clarity and awareness. By their very nature, some activities arouse a mental state of carelessness and heedlessness and therefore are not compatible with a meditative state or the Meditative Path.

For this reason, it often happens that as we become more interested in and committed to developing the path of peace and clarity, we avoid some counterproductive activities. This does not mean that we will become hermits or lead angelic lives. But we may choose to avoid the less conducive aspects and adopt a healthier lifestyle.

CHAPTER EIGHT

EXPLORING THE FIELDS
OF CONSCIOUSNESS

WE HAVE EXAMINED VARIOUS APPROACHES TO cultivating awareness and concentration using formal meditation techniques as well as the more informal method of Meditation in Action. If you have been practicing these techniques, you have no doubt become more familiar with both the workings of the mind and the nature of life. With this familiarity as a base, you can start to use your developing powers of awareness and concentration to investigate the nature of conscious experience itself.

Socrates said, "An unexamined life is a life not lived well." I would add that without systematic and careful investigation of our experiences in life, we can never arrive at true understanding and freedom. A foundation of awareness and concentration makes the mind fit for this journey. Without this foundation, investigations into the nature of conscious experience often lead only to excessive thinking, speculation, and confusion.

When asked how much concentration a practitioner should develop before embarking on the path of investigation, my teacher would say, "Enough to do the work!" Try to remember that meaningful insights can only arise in a peaceful mind. That "rule of thumb" can help you decide the direction for your practice at any time.

YOU ARE THE CENTER OF YOUR UNIVERSE

Let us begin by examining how we experience the world. Each of us is the center of our own universe, and the world we experience is a subjective one. Trying to be objective about something means that we strive to think rationally about it, to understand it from different perspectives. However, no matter how objective we try to be, our perception will still be a subjective experience, because we are at the center of any objective process. We can talk about a "world out there," but the only world we can know directly is the one we experience subjectively through our consciousness or mind. As Wayne Teasdale puts it:

> The perception of an external world, the existence of others, even the fact of our own bodies, are presented

and represented to us through the agency of our consciousness. . . . We are unable to get outside the "skin"
of our consciousness to experience what might be there.
(*The Mystic Heart*, 65-66)

What, then, does the world consist of? For each of us, it
consists of what we have experienced in life until now and what
we can expect to experience in the future. The variety of our
possible experiences may seem so vast that it defies description
or classification. While this impression may be true in the sense
that each moment of life is unique, in a more general sense, our
experience of life is quite limited.

If we are blessed with a full complement of functioning
sense organs, our world is made up of six fields of experience:
whatever we can see, hear, taste, smell, touch, and think about.
These sense experiences constitute all that there is to our world,
because we experience life only through our senses. There are
five external sense organs—eyes, ears, nose, tongue, and
body—and one internal sense organ—the mind—without
which no conscious experience of any sort is possible.

In the West, we often speak of only the five physical senses
and fail to recognize that the mind is also a "sense door." Not
only does the mind make possible the act of conscious experience through the external senses, but it also allows us to be con-

scious of purely mental experiences in the form of abstract concepts, ideas, and emotions. When I listed the six fields of experience above, I used the word "think" in a very loose manner for
the sake of simplicity. To be more accurate and comprehensive,
the field of consciousness perceived through the mind consists
of a variety of "mental phenomena," including such positive and
negative mental states and emotions as patience, confidence,
regard for others, pride, and jealousy. Mental phenomena also
include experiences of joy unrelated to thinking or any perception of the external sensory world such as those experienced by
people who have achieved refined levels of concentration.

The fields of perception we can access through the six kinds
of sense consciousness are the extent of our subjective world.
Eyes make it possible for us to see visible objects of an endless
variety of colors and shapes. But regardless of the specific
details, our conscious experience will simply be that of seeing.
The same is true with the other senses, so that through the ears
we experience hearing, the tongue allows for tasting, and the
nose facilitates smelling.

The body itself is a sense organ because its many nerve end-
ings allow us to experience touch of various types, including
hard and soft, hot and cold, rough and smooth. Of course, the
mind or mental consciousness is the necessary "screen" against
which all other sense experiences manifest. When there is no

other object of experience manifesting on the screen of the mind, but awareness is still active, then mind consciousness consists of a bright and clear screen which represents a very pure mental state.

How We Experience the World

As was mentioned earlier, the mind, or consciousness, moves extremely quickly from one object to another. In Buddhist scriptures it is said that a moment of consciousness is of inconceivably short duration, lasting only a billionth part of the time it takes for lightening to flash in the sky.

Because consciousness moves so quickly, we seem to be experiencing several things simultaneously. Thus, while we are watching a movie, we seem to be able to see the action on the screen, hear all the sound effects and dialogue, and taste the popcorn we are eating all at the same time. However, if we were to pay very careful attention with sufficiently sharp awareness, we may discover that our impression of simultaneous experience is faulty and that the nature of our conscious experience is quite different.

In some Eastern meditation traditions in which the introspective exploration of the mind is highly refined, it is taught that during a moment in which we are actually seeing, it is not possible to hear anything. The same is true for the other senses. At any moment, these traditions hold, we can be conscious of only one sense experience. However, as there is nothing faster than the movement of consciousness, we experience life as a dynamic, flowing process of simultaneous experiences. If this were not the case, we would have a terrible time trying to cope with life!

It is also important to understand that regardless of which sense door facilitates an experience, that experience is always accompanied by a feeling. The word *feeling* as used here does not mean an emotion or any complex mental reaction, but rather a very basic and fundamental "tone" or quality associated with each experience. This feeling is purely subjective. It automatically characterizes each experience as being pleasant, unpleasant, or neutral in nature.

How we react to any experience will be primarily determined by whether the associated feeling is pleasant, unpleasant, or neutral. Our instinctual and conditioned reaction will always be to chase after pleasant experiences, avoid unpleasant ones, and ignore the neutral experiences in life.

In summary, we can describe our experience of the world in the following way:

When a sense door comes into contact with a sense object, the consciousness registers an experience characterized by a pleasant, unpleasant, or neutral feeling. Thus:

- Eyes and visible objects lead to seeing and a pleasant, unpleasant, or neutral feeling.
- Ears and sounds lead to hearing and a pleasant, unpleasant, or neutral feeling.
- Tongue and tastes lead to tasting and a pleasant, unpleasant, or neutral feeling.
- Nose and odors lead to smelling and a pleasant, unpleasant, or neutral feeling.
- Body and tactile objects lead to touching and a pleasant, unpleasant, or neutral feeling.
- Mind and mind objects lead to mental phenomena and a pleasant, unpleasant, or neutral feeling.

BEING A GOOD STUDENT

Describing the world in this matter-of-fact way is not intended to detract from the richness of life or the uniqueness of any experience. Its purpose is to help us investigate the nature of consciousness so that we can see life more clearly and understand why we react to it the way we do. When we use the awareness and concentration we have developed to look more clearly at how we experience the world, the practice of meditation unfolds into a process of insightful realizations that can lead to change, growth, and freedom.

As I discovered through my own experience, investigating the nature of sense consciousness can help us advance in our meditation practice. In my early years of training, I did not always live in the same monastery as my teacher, because Ajahn Chah was responsible for a large number of monasteries. During one such period, I was having some difficulty in my practice, and I greatly missed my teacher's guidance. When I next had the opportunity to see him, I complained about not having a teacher at the place where I was staying. He listened to me patiently and with great kindness said, "But you do have a teacher. In fact, you have six teachers—your eyes, ears, nose, tongue, body, and mind. These are your teachers. However, you need to be a good student in order to learn."

In the following chapters, we continue our journey of exploration by examining our usual reactions to life's experiences more closely. The way we relate to people and respond to situations shapes our lives. Therefore, we need to be "good students" in order to find the path to inner peace and outer harmony.

Exercise: Exploring the Six Fields of Consciousness

As my teacher advised, it is worthwhile to spend some time exploring the six fields of conscious experience to become more familiar with them. To facilitate this process, I suggest the following exercises that include both formal and informal meditation:

A Walk in the Park

A walk in the park offers an excellent opportunity to explore the world through each of the senses. Choose a pleasant day when you have time to visit a forest preserve or a quiet park and try this exercise.

Begin by centering yourself and encourage the mind to become calm and quiet. Then open your mind to the visual world by being aware of the natural sights before you. Notice the different shades of green, the dark colors of the tree trunks, and the blue sky. If you see a flower, look at its intricate shape and delicate colors. With silent awareness, experience fully the numerous shapes and colors that make up the visible world.

Now, stand still for a while and feel the breeze on your cheeks and the pressure of the ground on the soles of your feet. This is the world of touch. Reach out and touch a leaf. Notice its texture. Walk up to a tree and put your hands on its trunk, feeling the roughness of the bark. Spend some time exploring the world of touch, silently aware of this field of experience.

Then notice the world of sounds all around you. Open your mind to this world by listening to the sounds of the wind in the trees, the chirping of the birds, and the rustling in the undergrowth. Sounds from close by and those from far away all come to you. Be very still and quiet within, staying receptive and transparent to this field of experience as sounds flow through you.

Remaining very quiet, turn your attention to the sense of smell. Become aware of the smells of nature, vegetation, the earth, or any scent in the air. If there is a fragrant bush or flower nearby, go to it and experience the fragrance fully, noticing how subtle, delicate, and fleeting the world of smell can be.

Of course, there is also the world of taste to be explored. How wonderful it would be to find a mulberry tree with juicy ripe fruit on its branches to savor! If you are not so lucky as to find such a tree on this walk, then bring out that box of raisins in your pocket and fully enjoy the taste as you eat them.

Thus far, you have used awareness to explore the world through your five physical senses. Now it is time to find a quiet place to rest, close your eyes, and bring your attention inward. Become aware of your inner world of mental activity. Is it noisy or busy in the mind? Listen to and observe this mental process, gradually thinning out the chatter by replacing it with a simple thought such as "peace and harmony." Continue to repeat this phrase gently in your mind, quietly listening and allowing these pleasant thoughts to calm your whole being.

To complete this exercise, you may want to practice Mindfulness of Breathing for a little while.

Meditation with Sound

I have found meditating on sound to be a very effective method for quieting a noisy mind. You may practice this type of meditation in two ways:

• Soothing music: A wide variety of music is available that is designed to promote calmness and tranquility. Such recordings often mix the sounds of nature with gentle and soothing music. Most tapes of this variety are suitable for practicing meditation on sound.

With the music playing at an agreeable volume, sit comfortably with your eyes closed. Put aside all other concerns, become very quiet, both physically and mentally, and open the mind to the world of sound that is around you. Listen to the soothing music as it flows through you, always changing as each moment gives birth to a new sound. Encourage the mind to remain in this state of inner silence, being completely open and receptive to the world of sound. Allow the music to calm and soothe every aspect of your being so that only the sound of the music exists in an inner ocean of peace.

This practice can be a very good way to calm and quiet the mind. However, you need to watch out for the hindrance of dullness, because it can easily sneak up on you during this type of meditation.

• Every sound and no sound: This exercise is highly effective for stilling and focusing the mind. The approach employed in this meditation technique reminds me of a movie I saw long ago. In one scene a duel took place between the hero, armed only with a knife, and the villain, who was armed with a sword. To make the duel more dramatic, the antagonists agreed that it should take place in a large and completely dark room.

Imagine what it would be like to be the hero in that pitch black room, knowing that there is another person in the space with a sword in his hand and an unfriendly intention in his mind! What do you think your mind would be doing . . . daydreaming or worrying about the weather? I am certain that your whole attention would be focused on one thing—listening for the slightest sound from any direction!

From this illustration you may appreciate the intensity of interest that can be developed in the world of sound. However, it would be very difficult to experience any peace in the situation in which that movie hero found himself. Therefore, I suggest that you try doing this exercise under more conducive conditions, when you feel comfortable and relaxed and do not have to worry about a villain with a sword!

For this exercise, follow the same procedure as in practicing Mindfulness of Breathing. When you feel settled, comfortable, and centered, turn your attention to the world of sounds. Keeping the mind very quiet, listen for any sound that may come to you: soft sounds that are close by and sounds from far away; sounds that are part of the background and sounds that come and go very quickly. Do not linger on any sound or chase after it. Simply remain very quiet and transparent. Allow the sounds to flow through the mind without any interference on your part. There is no need to label or describe, recognize or analyze. Just hear each sound with interest and awareness.

Remain alert, vigilant, and receptive, because sounds can come from any direction at any moment. If there are no sounds, then listen to "the sound of silence." Within the peaceful and quiet mind, it is possible to hear both sounds and silence with

equal clarity. Finish the meditation with a period of Mindfulness
of Breathing.

QUESTION TIME

Normal living involves many things happening so fast that the type of atten-
tion to experience you describe seems impossible. Is it really necessary to be
aware of every moment of experience?

Life is a complex and fast-flowing series of events moving through the mind. If we think of practicing awareness as requiring that we identify the contents of every
moment, it would be impossible for us to function normally. However, we do not practice being aware in this
rigorous way.

Assuming that at present you are sitting, how will you
manage to stand up and walk? If you had to think about
every movement of the muscles involved in walking,
you would never be able to rise from your seat.
However, simply by arousing the intention to stand and
walk, you can easily accomplish this complex task.

Similarly, it is possible for us to relax into the present,

remaining centered and awake while going about our normal lives. When there is something to be done, we do it. When there is a problem to be solved, we solve it in the best possible way. When there is nothing to do, we rest in peace.

The way to practice awareness in daily life was succinctly expressed by a Chinese master in this stanza:

If you walk, just walk.
If you sit, just sit.
But don't wobble!
(Timothy Freke, *Zen Wisdom*, 67)

You have stated that a person's range of experience is limited to what can be known through the six senses. What about the mystical experiences that some people have?

When talking about "mystical experiences," people often refer to a great many things ranging from the sublime to the ridiculous. Sometimes they describe seeing unusual images or hearing voices to which they give special significance. Other experiences can be associated with altered states of consciousness brought about through some form of meditation or contemplation or by other means. Again, the interpretation a person assigns to any such experience will depend upon individual understanding and beliefs.

It is not appropriate for me or anyone else to interpret the validity or significance of these different forms of experience. However, regardless of the specific nature of any mystical experience, it is received through one of the six senses. Even communion with the most sublime and beautiful state of Oneness, be it Ultimate Reality or God, is only possible through the sense door of the mind.

CHAPTER NINE

༺✺༒

WORKING WITH PAIN

IN THE LAST CHAPTER, WE SAW THAT OUR subjective world is made up of six fields of conscious experience and that each moment of experience elicits a pleasant, unpleasant, or neutral feeling. Feelings alone, however, are not what determines the quality of life. Of far greater importance than the feeling associated with any experience is the way we choose to respond to that feeling. An experience may be pleasant or unpleasant, but it is what we do with these feelings that makes for an elated or miserable state of mind.

This chapter examines the physical experience of pain and our reaction to it as an example of how this principle works. We apply the same principle on a broader scale in the following chapter.

THE BODY IS LIKE AN OPEN DOOR

Having a physical body that is functioning normally means that we are exposed to sensations throughout life. Naturally, we wish to experience pleasurable physical sensations as much as possible and avoid anything that is in the slightest way unpleasant, uncomfortable, or painful. Unfortunately, having a body sensitive to pleasant sensations automatically implies that we are subject to the opposite experience. The sense door of the body is similar to any other door. Once it is open, anyone can walk through, friend or foe. Thus, the consequence of being receptive to physical pleasure is that we are at times exposed to pain and discomfort. Such is the nature of life.

All living creatures have an instinctual bias for pleasant feelings. This drive is part of a survival mechanism that pushes us toward self-gratification and self-preservation. At this instinctual level, our reactions are not different from those of a cat or a dog. Even plants exhibit a similar tendency. Have you ever observed how a plant or flower inclines and grows toward its source of light? In the case of plants, this tendency may not be a conscious choice, but the underlying drive is the same. Moving toward the source of heat and light gratifies the plant's needs for growth and survival.

It is natural and healthy for us to prefer pleasant physical experiences, since discomfort or pain often indicates conditions threatening to our well-being or survival. However, because human beings have developed a capacity for thinking, analyzing, imagining, and planning far beyond the basic instincts we share with other animals, it is possible for us to react to experiences in more complex ways. Depending upon how we use our highly developed intellect, we can react to pain in ways either much better or much worse than ordinary animals.

THE NEGATIVE REACTION TO PAIN CAUSES MISERY

Let's look more closely at the experience of pain. Because pain is subjective, a very painful experience for one person might cause only minor discomfort for another. In fact, there is no way to know directly how "painful" someone else's migraine or toothache actually is. Despite these differences, we all experience some pain. The question is, what do we do with the experience? When we are faced with a painful feeling, is our ability to think an advantage or a disadvantage?

Let me answer this question by telling a story from my own experience. While in Western Australia, I lived in a forest monastery which was also home to many wild kangaroos. One cold winter day, I was sitting in my hut with a blanket wrapped around me trying to stay warm. I looked out the window to see a number of kangaroos grazing in the forest. Although it was raining heavily and a cold wind was blowing, the kangaroos just continued to graze.

I thought to myself, "Those kangaroos must be feeling really miserable out there in that cold rain."

What I was doing, of course, was putting myself into the "kangaroos' shoes" and assuming that they were preoccupied with thoughts like mine. "What a miserable life this is," I could imagine them thinking. "Completely unfair! Why does that human get to sit in a warm, dry hut while I am out here in the cold? Why does it have to rain so much while I am trying to eat? It'll probably rain all day, and I'll get pneumonia and die from it!"

But then I realized that the kangaroos were not thinking those thoughts at all. Surely, they felt some physical discomfort from the rain and cold, but they were not creating more mental anguish by worrying about how long it was going to rain or the possibility of their getting pneumonia. I knew that if the kangaroos were to find a safe and dry place, they might seek refuge from the wet and cold. However, as no such place was readily available, they simply continued to eat without making a big problem out of their uncomfortable situation.

This story illustrates an important truth. When we are confronted with pain and discomfort, we human beings often experience far more mental anguish than animals because of the way we dwell upon our situation. The world may cause us to be uncomfortable, but we make ourselves miserable with thinking based upon fear, anxiety, and aversion. Our highly developed ability to think can, in this case, become a cause for greater suffering.

How does this process work? When we humans experience physical pain, we naturally do not like it and so want to get rid of it. If we cannot eliminate the experience of pain immediately, we start worrying that it may last a long time, possibly get worse, and eventually become dangerous. In addition to the original pain, we experience fear and anxiety. This unhappy state of mind results in misery and suffering much more intense than the pain that triggered it. We have transformed a simple feeling of pain into an oppressive state of mental anguish. Of course, this negative state of mind also affects the body by causing stress, which signals the muscles to tense up. This tension may result in greater physical pain. Noticing that the pain is indeed becoming worse, we react with even more aversion, fear, and anxiety, making the whole experience unbearable.

This negative reaction to pain is a "vicious cycle," because once we start on this path, even minor physical discomfort can be transformed into an oppressive state of mental suffering that leads, in turn, to even more physical pain. However, we need not react in this self-destructive way to unpleasant physical sensations. There are more skillful modes of response open to us.

Positive Ways of Responding to Pain

In an earlier chapter, I mentioned that when faced with an unpleasant or disturbing experience, we can respond in one of three ways:

- Remove the cause of the unpleasant or disturbing experience.
- Ignore the experience completely.
- Coexist peacefully with the experience without any negative reaction.

These same three options apply when we must choose an appropriate response to discomfort and pain. It is worthwhile to examine each option so that we can understand how and when to use them.

Removing the Cause of Discomfort and Pain

This option is often our first response to an uncomfortable sensation, and it is an appropriate one. Pain usually signals that something is "wrong," in the sense that the body is under stress or exposed to some form of harmful contact. The logical response is to act to protect the body from damage. Thus, if you accidentally touch something hot, the feeling of physical pain causes you to pull back your hand immediately to avoid being burned.

When pain arises, we should consider it a warning of possible danger to the body, investigate the cause, and apply a suitable remedy. If we feel "pangs of hunger," we relieve that discomfort by eating. When we have a headache, we take medicine or apply a cold compress to help ease the pain. However, it is important that we avoid using a remedy that leads to greater problems later on, or err by choosing a cure that is worse than the disease.

For instance, a blacksmith was busily at work beating and shaping a hot piece of metal. While both of his hands were occupied, a big blowfly landed on his forehead. The blacksmith's son was standing close by. "Son," the blacksmith said, "this blowfly is really annoying me! Please get rid of it." Eager to help, the little boy picked up a hammer and smashed the fly on his father's forehead! Needless to say, for many days the poor blacksmith had a headache that annoyed him much more than any blowfly.

This little story illustrates that we should use our intelligence and resources to alleviate physical pain and discomfort in the world but that we must be careful not to create worse problems in the process for others, for the environment, or for ourselves. It is also important to realize that we can never eliminate completely all forms of discomfort and pain. As long as the body remains a sensitive organ for experiencing contact, life will always include some unpleasant physical feelings.

Unfortunately, because we rely so heavily on our ability to remove the causes of pain, we have, in fact, reduced our tolerance for pain and thus made ourselves more vulnerable. The slightest discomfort has the power to intimidate us; even the thought of experiencing pain can make life unbearable. I remember my first visits to the dentist as an excruciating experience—not because of the physical pain, which was relatively minor, but because of my fear and anxiety.

It is not necessary for us to live in fear of pain that has not yet arisen or to be helpless victims of pain and discomfort that is unavoidable. So let us consider the other options available to us for dealing with pain.

Ignoring the Discomfort or Pain Completely

Although physical pain is nature's way of warning us about possible harm so that we can protect the body, there are times when the most appropriate action—and often the only option—is simply to ignore the pain. For example, if you develop a headache or toothache while driving home through a snowstorm, you may need to ignore the pain and apply yourself fully to completing your journey safely.

We also often ignore discomfort or pain when we are involved in something that we find very interesting. Many years ago, for example, I had a case of laryngitis and a very sore throat. To make matters worse, at the time I was on a long trip on an airplane in which the air was very dry. For the first hour, I coughed, swallowed, or cleared my throat every few minutes. Though my condition was not serious or dangerous in any way, it was painful, and I was feeling quite miserable. Then the in-flight movie came on. By chance, it was a science fiction film that I had not seen. Being a big fan of science fiction, I soon became completely engrossed in the movie. I did not even remember my painful throat until the end of the film. In effect, for the hour or two during which I watched the movie, science fiction "cured" me. I felt no pain or irritation and was free of the urge to cough or the need to swallow. My sore throat was of no consequence, because I completely ignored it.

It is certainly possible for us to turn our attention away from a painful sensation when we are motivated to do so for one reason or another. Of course, we may also learn to develop this ability through the practice of meditation. For instance, while practicing Mindfulness of Breathing, we intentionally ignore other objects of attention, including physical discomfort or pain, and arouse interest only in the breath. Once we have achieved some degree of concentration, it is relatively easy for us to keep the attention exclusively on the breath so that the experience of physical pain does not arise in the mind.

I have seen for myself how effective this technique can be. While in Australia, I had a student who was afflicted with an extremely painful form of arthritis that flared up at different times. His condition motivated him to become quite an accomplished meditator and to develop good concentration using Mindfulness of Breathing. He found that during the meditation period, he could temporarily achieve complete relief from his pain.

People with chronic pain must often learn to ignore the painful sensations. Obviously, they first seek relief through various skillful means, including medication and physical therapy. However, having exhausted such means, they often turn their attention to other things, even though pain continues to be present. Many people have found the inner strength to live normal and rewarding lives in spite of pain. We can all use this method of dealing with pain on occasions when it is appropriate or necessary. If there is no other choice, we simply get on with living, just as those kangaroos got on with grazing on a cold and wet winter day.

Coexisting Peacefully with Pain

So far we have discussed the options of removing the causes of pain and ignoring the pain. When we are successful in using either of these methods, we are no longer conscious of the experience of pain. However, through the power of awareness and concentration, it is also possible for us to coexist peacefully with pain by embracing it in consciousness without creating anguish or suffering in the mind. In this approach, physical pain itself becomes the object of meditation and contemplation.

Meditation on pain can empower us by releasing the mind from unnecessary fear. Training in this method does not require doing anything harmful to the body. Rather, it applies the meditative mind to the common physical discomforts that we experience.

Having already developed some degree of awareness, we are able to notice what the mind is doing and to understand the thinking with which it is preoccupied. Furthermore, through training in concentration, we have gained some skill at directing and focusing our attention. This focus gives us a degree of control over our thought process; we can choose what to think about and how to think about it. As a result, we are now in position to explore the possibility of changing the habitual "vicious cycle" of negative reaction to pain.

For the purpose of this discussion, let us assume that we are faced with a physical pain that cannot be avoided, such as a headache that is not responding to medication we have taken.

The normal tendency is to start a negative mental cycle by dwelling on thoughts motivated by fear and aversion: "Maybe this headache will get worse. Maybe it will never stop. Maybe it's not a headache, but a brain tumor!" However, with awareness, we can recognize this movement in the mind and, with concentration, we can stop the process. Instead of allowing the mind to continue to think along those lines, we intentionally bring the attention back to the bare experience of the physical sensation as it is in that very moment. Rather than "thinking about" the pain, we establish a state of awareness in which the mind is peacefully coexisting with—not reacting to—the physical feeling.

Simple, unembellished physical pain is usually quite bearable. Any pain that you or I have experienced must have been bearable, otherwise we would be dead. What makes pain seem unbearable is thinking about how bad it is going to be, how long it is going to last, or how dangerous it is. All of that mental proliferation and speculation can transform the bare physical sensation of pain into an ominous monster.

If we can stop the mind from entering into that negative reactive cycle, we retain our inner poise and serenity despite the presence of physical pain. To do this, we simply sustain the awareness and concentration that keeps the mind quietly present, conscious of the bare sensation from moment to moment.

It is not a matter of gritting our teeth to endure hours of excruciating pain. We need only remain aware of and be at peace
with the physical sensation of pain in this one moment. Of
course, if we can bear the pain for one moment, we can do it for
any moment. We discover that it is possible for the peaceful
mind to embrace physical discomfort with no disruption of that
peace.

Furthermore, by not creating unnecessary mental anguish
with negative thoughts of fear and aversion, we do not place
our bodies under further stress. The muscles do not tense, and
the physical pain is not magnified. In fact, we often find that if
the mind is peacefully coexisting with pain, the physical feeling
itself will change or even dissolve.

It is certainly worthwhile to develop the skill to use awareness and concentration in this way. The next time you find
yourself faced with some physical discomfort, take the opportunity to practice this meditation. Here are a few occasions
when you might practice this valuable technique:

- *Meditating in a hot bus*: Sitting in a hot, stuffy bus can be
  quite unpleasant. Instead of allowing the mind to get
  all worked up with such negative thoughts as "Why
  don't they fix the air conditioning? My good suit will
  be soaked in sweat by the time I get to the office. I
  can't stand this heat!" stop and establish awareness.

Why should your mind become hot just because the body is hot? Try to center yourself and turn your attention to the bare physical sensations in the body. See if you can keep the mind very quiet, remaining at peace with the physical discomfort by not reacting to it. Peacefully coexist with the heat. This discomfort in the present moment is definitely bearable.

As the mind calms down, you may find that the body relaxes and actually begins to cool down. Instead of having to endure a hot body and a hot mind, you discover that it is possible to have a hot body and a cool mind, which may lead to a cool body, even when it's sitting in a hot bus.

• *Meditating at the dentist*: It is not pleasant to have someone working in your mouth, especially if that work involves drilling and the like. However, the actual physical discomfort is not as bad as you may imagine it to be. On your next visit to the dentist, try to center yourself by making the mind calm and quiet. Relax all the muscles in your body, especially those around your face. Because there will be an automatic tendency to tense up, continually bring the attention to the body, and try to release and relax any unnecessary tightness. By keeping the mind involved with the body in this way, you will find any physical discomfort to be quite bearable.

• *Meditating at the health club*: Strenuous exercise of any form will naturally be somewhat painful. Many people working out at health clubs deal with this pain by distracting themselves by watching television or listening to music. In fact, these people are using the second option discussed above for dealing with their physical discomfort. They are ignoring pain by turning their attention to something else that they find interesting.

However, I do not consider this option to be the best approach in this situation. When the muscles are being worked during strenuous exercise, the body is under considerable stress. Not paying attention to the body under these circumstances may result in overexertion or injury. Therefore, I think it is preferable to give full attention to physical feelings during any vigorous exercise.

For instance, if you are running on a treadmill, it is best to remain fully aware of the body, noticing what it feels like and releasing any unnecessary tension in the muscles. At whatever speed you are running, you should try to find a rhythm that requires the least amount of exertion. If the mind is centered in the body, it is caring for the body and peacefully coexisting with any feelings of pain or discomfort that are present. While running in this way, the body will not tire as quickly because you are not wasting physical energy. In addition, you are reducing your chances of accidental injury.

UNDERSTANDING OUR OPTIONS

If we use these and the other occasions in ordinary life when we face pain and discomfort as opportunities for practicing meditation, we can empower ourselves so that physical pain no longer causes us fear and anxiety.

Because pain is a fact of life, it is important that we understand our options for dealing with it. Through our intellect, awareness, and concentration, we can choose the best possible response to any situation. We need not be helpless victims of circumstances or remain at the mercy of our own negative thoughts.

We can be better than a cat or a dog—even better than those kangaroos. In fact, if we develop our full potential, we may realize a state of freedom that allows us to say with complete confidence, "The world may make me uncomfortable, but it can never make me miserable!"

Exercise: Standing like a Mountain

In one of the monasteries where I lived, it was required that we practice standing meditation for at least an hour at a time. I confess that I never developed a liking for this form of meditation practice, but it is very effective for learning to work with pain. It is also useful for improving posture and helping to still the busy mind. Therefore, I encourage you to try practicing the following meditation exercise for a period of about twenty minutes.

Establish the same conditions as for a period of sitting meditation. Remove your shoes and stand up straight with your feet flat on the floor. Keep your feet parallel and about two inches apart. Gently close your eyes and become aware of the body standing still. Check to see that the legs are straight and tighten the buttocks a little. The rest of the back should be erect, following the natural shape of the spine. The neck is straight, and the top of the head is reaching toward the ceiling. The ears are in line with the shoulders. Allow the arms to hang loosely by your sides.

Now, while keeping your feet flat on the floor, try to grow as tall as you can with the top of the head reaching up toward the sky. Let the body breathe as it wants, and do not concern yourself with the breathing. Only experience the body standing erect and tall. Try to find your balance so that the weight of the body is evenly distributed over the soles of the feet. Stand quite still and very tall. Gradually release any unnecessary tension in the body, but try to keep the body erect.

Remain aware of this erect posture with your attention centered along a vertical axis passing through the top of your head all the way through the body to a point between your two feet. If the mind is very quiet and aware of the erect posture, the body will be perfectly still. As soon as your mind starts drifting into thoughts or distractions, you will notice the body swaying a little, and there will be a corresponding shift of pressure on the soles of the feet. So try to remain very quiet by keeping the mind fully with the body, silently standing still.

Stand like a tall, solid mountain, with its peak high in the sky and its base solidly embedded in the earth. Such a mountain stands firm and unmoving.

As you continue to stand in this manner, it is natural for some discomfort or pain to arise in the feet, shins, or other part of the body. Because these feelings are not dangerous to your health, they are suitable objects for practicing meditation on pain. Therefore, when any pain begins to arise, avoid moving, and continue to stand very still. Direct your attention to the physical sensation of discomfort, and keep the mind very quiet, not fighting the pain or running away from it. Simply remain aware of the pain as a physical sensation in the present moment.

- What is this sensation like?

- Is it hot or cold?

- Is it constant in nature or does it change and move?

Try to sustain this quality of nonreactive awareness, peacefully coexisting with any unpleasant physical feeling without transforming it into a monster. Within the peaceful mind, the bare sensations of pain and discomfort are only vibrations that arise and pass away from moment to moment. Your underlying peace of mind is not disturbed by the physical sensations, just like the rocks in a creek bed are not disturbed by water flowing over them.

At the end of the meditation period, relax by stretching and bending your legs, and take a few moments to reflect upon your experience.

QUESTION TIME

If I remember correctly, you said earlier that it is better to meditate in a comfortable posture so as not to be distracted by pain. Is that advice no longer valid?

If you are practicing meditation with the primary purpose of cultivating the qualities of awareness, concentration, and serenity, then it is certainly advisable to establish the most favorable conditions. In Mindfulness of Breathing, for example, it is best to sit in a comfortable posture so that the mind can remain attentive to the breath more easily. I encourage you to continue developing skill at this type of training because it will help you establish and maintain a good foundation of awareness and concentration.

Meditation on pain requires that we utilize these qualities of awareness and concentration to examine the nature of physical pain and the way the mind reacts to it. The primary goal in this practice is to develop understanding and free the mind of some of its negative tendencies. In this case, the experience of pain or discomfort becomes the object of our attention and investigation. Therefore, it is considered a teacher rather than a distraction.

I have heard of people walking on red-hot coals without feeling any pain. Is that a type of mind control?

People can enter into altered states of consciousness in which they do not feel physical pain. These can be induced by various means, including hypnosis, meditation, and devotional practices. Under some extraordinary circumstances, such a state can even arise spontaneously in the mind. An example of this would be a soldier in the midst of a battle who is able to continue fighting without feeling pain, even after being severely wounded.

The power of the mind is far greater than we realize or utilize. However, the real goal of meditation is to discover the miracle of being fully awake and at peace while walking on ordinary surfaces.

I can accept that it is feasible to achieve certain states of mind in which we do not feel any physical pain, but is it possible to prevent physical damage to the body during that time?

Your state of mind greatly affects physical conditions in the body, including blood circulation, breathing, muscle contraction, as well as many other physiological functions. Therefore, with sufficiently developed mental ability, it may be possible to alter the normal physical processes to some extent. For instance, you may be able to prevent a wound from bleeding by intentionally restricting blood flow to that part of the body or learn to generate internal body heat to counteract the effects of excessive cold.

Again, we must appreciate that the mind is a marvelous phenomenon of tremendous power. Nevertheless, the body is a physical object consisting of ordinary matter, and regardless of the power of the mind, there is a limit to what the body can endure without being damaged.

CHAPTER TEN

CHANGING ANGER INTO LOVING KINDNESS

W E HAVE BEEN EXPLORING HOW TO USE THE qualities of awareness and concentration to examine our experiences and observe our reactions to them. This aspect of the Meditative Path helps us understand ourselves and provides an opportunity for change and growth. In the last chapter, we investigated the experience of physical pain to show how meditation can be used to improve our quality of life. We can use a similar process to free the mind gradually from other negative states that interfere with inner peace or outer harmony. This chapter examines how to use the process of meditative awareness to investigate and overcome a range of negative mental states that can be grouped under the heading of "anger."

WHAT IS ANGER?

Generally speaking, anger is a mental reaction that makes us want to strike out against an experience that is not pleasing to us. This reaction can vary in intensity from a feeling of irritation to a state of violent rage. Thus, anger may manifest as any one of a number of negative emotions, including irritation, annoyance, aversion, resentment, rage, and even hatred.

Although some people experience such states of mind more often than others, it is rare to find an individual who does not experience one or more of these reactions on a daily basis. Most people find a good part of life to be irritating, and many things that happen cause them to become quite angry. The worst form of this affliction is when the feeling of anger towards a person, situation, or event becomes a chronic reaction in the mind. We can tell that we are experiencing this problem if, long after an experience has caused us feelings of anger, we fall into a similar mental state whenever we are reminded of that experience. When we habitually react this way, our anger might be called resentment or hatred.

Of course, there is a vast difference between a feeling of mild irritation and the more violent response of rage. However, the difference lies not in the kind, but in the intensity of the reaction. Although the fire produced by a single match is less intense than a forest fire, both involve a similar process of combustion and share similar characteristics. Both, we might say, can burn us. Similarly, the various negative states within the spectrum of anger involve the same fundamental mental process and share a common characteristic: they cause outer conflict and destroy inner peace.

How Does Anger Arise?

It is not uncommon for us to say things like "You make me angry!" or "These children have been annoying me all day!" or "My boss is a very irritating person!" Such expressions reflect our inner belief that things or people "out there" make us angry. But does this interpretation of our experience reflect an accurate observation of reality? If people and events in the world truly had the power to make us angry, we would be no better than helpless victims. Fortunately, investigation shows that this is not the case.

Let's consider, for example, our response to some style of music, say "rap" or "country." If a particular kind of music were annoying in itself, then it would annoy everyone who hears it. But we find that while some people consider rap or country music to be annoying, others find it pleasing. Even the same person may find a kind of music annoying at certain times but not on other occasions. Is it possible, then, that music is simply sound and that the reaction of being annoyed or pleased by it is purely a subjective response of the listener?

If we use the light of awareness to investigate our experiences carefully, we discover that irritation and anger are always our own creations. True, the various experiences in life may be pleasing or not pleasing, but our internal response to any experience will depend upon how we think about it. In the case of pain, we saw how thinking based on fear can transform an unpleasant physical feeling into an oppressive state of mental anguish. A similar process can occur whenever we encounter any experience that does not please us. Reacting with negative thoughts creates a negative state of mind. Unfortunately, many experiences in life do not please us; thus we are often afflicted by anger and similar negative mental states.

Each individual has preferences and biases based upon physical and mental conditioning. Depending upon these preferences, we judge every experience to be pleasing, not pleasing, or neutral in nature. The example above helps us appreciate that people have different likes and dislikes about music, and the same holds true for everything else in life. People form individual preferences and biases about many aspects of the physical world, including food, the environment, weather, customs and behavior, or more abstract religious, philosophical, and aesthetic matters. The old proverb, "One man's meat is another man's poison" is an apt description of the subjective nature of all experience.

We all have our preferences that determine whether we deem an experience pleasing or otherwise. Our inclination is to pursue those experiences that we find pleasing and to avoid the opposite. However, given that we can never completely avoid experiences that do not please us, how are we to deal with the unpleasant ones? Our habitual tendency is to react with thoughts of aversion, such as, "I don't like this. It's not fair. How dare they do this to me? I'll show them!" By dwelling on such negative thoughts, we create mental states of anger and resentment. Here is how the Buddhist scriptures describe the consequences of this way of thinking:

> "He was angry with me; he attacked me; he defeated me; he robbed me"— those who dwell on such thoughts will never be free from hatred. (*The Dhammapada*, translated by Eknath Easwaran, 78)

In reality, no situation or person can make us angry; we make ourselves angry by perpetuating thoughts of aversion when faced with something that's not to our liking. *This realization has a profound implication: Because anger is our own creation, we have power over it.* We can stop creating anger and be free from its consequences. All we need to do is arouse the aspiration to achieve freedom and use the appropriate skillful means to attain it.

ANGER: FRIEND OR FOE?

How can we motivate ourselves to overcome anger? We might begin by considering the nature of anger to see whether it is a necessary, helpful, or pleasant state of mind. In other words, does anger improve the quality of our lives in any way?

If we have ever observed how our mind and body feel when we are angry, we will have no illusions about anger being a pleasant experience. Irritation, annoyance, and hatred are miserable states. Not only is the mind agitated so that we cannot rest, but the body is also affected in a negative way. It is well-known that a predisposition to anger and irritation contributes to many health problems, such as high blood pressure, digestive disorders, and stress-related illnesses.

Allowing for the fact that anger is a miserable state of mind and that it is detrimental to our health, does it have any redeeming value? Perhaps you think that anger can motivate people to "do what needs to be done." Indeed, anger can be a strong and energetic motivator, but it often compromises our performance because it weakens our reason, intelligence, carefulness, and circumspection. Whatever we do when we are angry, in other words, may fall short of our true potential.

For example, if you are engaged in any kind of negotiation, say a discussion with your boss over a raise you have asked for, the worst thing you can do is become angry. Anger can make you "lose your cool" and start blurting out all sorts of nonsense. You might even insult your boss and jeopardize your job. Whatever happens, it's unlikely that you'll get the raise you are seeking. While anger may be an effective motivator for irrational, foolish, and destructive action, it is not useful for improving the quality of our lives.

Other people might argue that "righteous indignation" or anger in response to some injustice in the world is a positive quality. We may have good reasons to justify our anger, and we may be right. But anger is never a constructive response that leads to beneficial action.

In many parts of rural Asia, people still use oxen-drawn carts to transport goods and produce. While standing on the side of the road, a man observed a merchant sitting on a fully laden cart being drawn by a scrawny ox. The merchant must have been in a hurry and impatient with the pace of the ox, for he was beating the poor animal with a whip. On seeing this act of cruelty, the man on the side of the road was overcome by feelings of indignation. He leapt onto the cart, grabbed the whip out of the merchant's hand, and started to beat him!

You may be thinking that the example above is remote from present-day experience, but consider the recent story of a father who had taken his ten-year-old son to play a game of hockey. Like many other sports, hockey can be quite aggressive, and it seems that this children's game was no exception. While watching from the stands, the father became increasingly angry by the amount of physical contact and fighting being tolerated by the adults monitoring the game. His righteous indignation focused on one of the men on the ice, who happened to be the parent of another player. The father became so irate that he assaulted the man as he was leaving the rink, and then, after being ordered out by a rink manger, returned to slam the man to the ground beside a soda machine. The man's head hit the concrete floor, killing him instantly.

As this shocking story illustrates, anger is not a constructive response to any situation. It is an affliction that benefits neither the person who is angry, nor the people who come into contact with that person. Even worse, anger tends to be contagious; it spreads easily from one person to another. Therefore, when we say, "I have a right to be angry!" we are saying in effect, "I have a right to suffer this miserable and destructive state of mind!" Indeed we do, but why would we want to exercise such a right?

We do not need anger to make a responsible and meaningful contribution to life. As human beings we can be motivated by more skillful qualities, such as reason, understanding, compassion, or duty. Anger is neither a good friend nor a helpful companion, so why not get rid of it?

FREEING THE MIND FROM THE AFFLICTION OF ANGER

If the preceding discussion has convinced you that anger is a state of mind you can do without, the Meditative Path offers a variety of approaches that can help you reduce the power of anger in your life. These methods help to free the mind from anger by changing the way you think about experiences, or the way you view the world.

Stopping the Cycle of Negative Thinking

We have already seen in the case of pain that it is possible for us to prevent the mind from sinking into a cycle of negative thinking when we are faced with an unpleasant physical sensation. We can apply the same approach to dealing with the anger that may arise when we come into contact with a person, experience, or situation that is not pleasing to us.

Using the awareness we have developed in meditation, we

can "catch ourselves" quickly when feelings and thoughts of irritation arise. At the first sign of an angry response, we halt the negative thinking by reminding ourselves that anger never solves anything and that it always contributes to misery. When we use our powers of awareness and concentration in this way, we are not repressing our anger; rather, we are making a conscious choice about how we wish to respond to a situation and the mental state we wish to create.

Buddhist teachers often say that dwelling on thoughts of anger is like picking up red-hot coals to throw at someone. Who will be burned first? Because we do not want to burn our own fingers, we stop ourselves from picking up the coals. Similarly, to prevent a mental state of misery, we stop the mind from indulging in thoughts of irritation and anger. We center ourselves and establish awareness to guard against such tendencies.

This approach can be quite effective if our awareness is sharp and we are able to catch the negative reaction at its inception, before it gathers momentum. However, once our reaction has developed into a strong feeling, it is very difficult to stop the process, because anger weakens the rational and reflective qualities of the mind. An angry mind is highly agitated and has little chance of establishing the clear awareness necessary to restore peace and balance.

We can think of anger, in this regard, as a fire in a wooded area and negative thoughts as the brush and other fuel that feeds the fire. While the fire is small, it is relatively easy to extinguish it by denying it fuel. However, once a brush fire has consumed enough fuel to grow into a forest fire, it is very difficult to put out. In such cases, firefighters often must retreat and establish a perimeter of firebreaks to contain the fire until it burns out.

Similarly, when anger has already developed into a strong emotion, it is very difficult for us to halt the negative mental cycle. We may need to retreat or remove ourselves from the situation until the inner fire of negative feelings and thoughts burns itself out. Then we will be able to reestablish awareness and assess the experience with a clear mind.

Replacing Negative Thoughts with Positive Ones

A variation on the approach above involves using awareness to interrupt negative thinking and replace it with constructive thoughts that help diffuse the feelings of irritation and annoyance. In other words, instead of continuing to justify and reinforce our negative reaction to a situation, we make the effort to bring to mind thoughts that elicit a more positive response.

We can prove to ourselves that this technique is effective by considering the following story: A man was waiting at the station for his usually punctual 7 o'clock train to the city. But this morning, the train was late. As he waited, the man became increasingly irate. By the time the train arrived forty minutes later, he was fuming. He could barely restrain himself from venting his anger at the conductor. However, before the man could speak, he overheard someone say that there had been an accident at the previous station during which a little girl had been killed. The feelings of sympathy and sorrow the man felt at this news caused his anger to vanish immediately.

Many times we generate anger or irritation about some situation based on assumptions and speculation because we do not know all the facts. Rather than persist in this unhappy pattern, we might try abstaining from judgment or giving people the benefit of the doubt until we understand what's really going on. To counter rising feelings of anger, we can intentionally bring to mind an explanation that helps us respond in a more patient and equanimous way.

For example, say you are driving to work and someone cuts in front of you. Instead of becoming angry or planting the seeds for "road rage" by indulging in negative thoughts about inconsiderate and dangerous drivers, why not give the driver who cut in front of you the benefit of the doubt? What if someone in that car was being rushed to the hospital? What if that driver was late to pick up a young child who was waiting at school? Once the thought of those possibilities arises in the mind, your feeling of annoyance automatically disappears.

The two methods for dealing with anger we have discussed—stopping the cycle of negative thinking and replacing
negative thoughts with positive ones—assume that we have sufficient awareness to catch our negative thoughts early in the
cycle, before they generate too much energy. Both are valuable
techniques that require continuous vigilance, like an allergy that
requires preventative medicine to keep its painful symptoms
from flaring up. Other approaches to anger focus more directly
on the root cause of the problem—the way we view ourselves
and the world around us.

Changing Our Attitude

Since our attitudes color the way we perceive the world, we
may be able to get at the root of anger by examining our view
of the world with the aim of replacing critical, impatient, and
intolerant attitudes with patient, tolerant, and forgiving ones.
When we do, we automatically find the world—and help to
make the world—a less irritating place.

First of all, most of us have highly developed critical faculties. That is to say, we have views and opinions about everything and everyone. Because of this tendency to judge, we are
continually deciding whether we approve of or like each experience as it occurs. Wherever we go and whatever we do, our

internal "critic" is saying, "I don't like this," or "I don't approve of that." Constant judging predisposes us to experience irritation, annoyance, and anger. I'm sure you can remember many times when your negative judgment or disapproval of even a trivial event—an umpire's call at a baseball game, an off-hand remark by a business associate—made you feel annoyed, irritated, or even angry.

The more intolerant and demanding we are, the more irritation and anger we experience. It is impossible to change the world so that nothing we encounter arouses our disapproval. Working consciously to reduce our tendency to judge and to soften our critical attitudes is the only solution. To make this point, my teacher would often tell the story of the mangy dog:

A dog with the mange sought relief from its affliction by running from one place to another. First, the dog would lie in the shade, but it would soon feel uncomfortable and go and lie in a bush. After a short time, it would feel the irritation again and run off to sit in the open. But nothing brought relief. Wherever the mangy dog went, it was miserable, because it was not the place or the conditions, but the disease that caused its discomfort. If it could be cured of the mange, the dog would be comfortable anywhere.

The dog's mange, of course, is a metaphor for any attitude

that causes us to react negatively and create misery. Changing our attitude to become less critical does not mean that we abandon our appreciation for good and bad, or right and wrong, and start living irresponsible lives. It simply means that we become a little more tolerant and patient. It is unrealistic to expect everything and everybody to be exactly as we want them to be at all times, and yet we often approach life with this attitude. Little wonder, then, that we experience so much irritation and anger!

A traditional example of the attitude we want to overcome is the story of the man who thought it would be marvelous to cover the whole earth with soft leather so that he could walk everywhere without hurting his tender feet. It was a nice idea, but completely impractical. A wiser man would make a pair of shoes that allowed him to walk wherever he liked without pain. We cannot change everything and control everybody to satisfy our whims and wishes. But we can change our attitudes and learn to accommodate a variety of conditions and situations without becoming upset, irritated, or angry.

My teacher would say to us, "Look at the trees in the forest. Do you see that some are big and tall while others are small, and that some are straight while others are crooked? People are like trees; you cannot expect them all to be the same." This teaching reminds us that if we can be a little more accommodating of the people around us, we experience less anger and conflict.

At other times, my teacher would hold up his hand and say, "Look at these fingers. They are all of different lengths and thicknesses, yet they can coexist in harmony, each fulfilling a purpose. Even this little pinky is useful for scratching inside the ear." Indeed, variety enriches life, and not everything needs to be the way we think it should be. By learning to allow for differences and to accommodate diversity, we reduce our risk for irritation and anger.

Another important attitude for diminishing negative states of mind is forgiveness. Either intentionally or through carelessness, we all make mistakes. Learning to accommodate human imperfections lessens our tendency to nurse grudges or harbor resentment and helps us forgive others as well as ourselves.

Forgiving mistakes does not mean that we condone mediocrity or evil. It only means that we are willing to allow a new start in the present with hope for the future. Forgiveness is a soothing ointment applied to a wound so that healing can take place. It is an essential part of a healthy attitude and conducive to a peaceful and harmonious life.

In his book *No Future Without Forgiveness*, the Reverend Desmond Tutu illustrates the healing effect of forgiveness with some very powerful examples. For instance, he tells the story of a mother whose seven-year-old daughter was kidnapped during a family camping trip in Montana. The kidnapper was eventually caught, but not in time to save the child's life. Even faced with such a horrible tragedy, Tutu reports, the mother refused to become a victim of hatred:

> Though I readily admit that initially I wanted to kill the man with my bare hands, by the time of the resolution of his crimes, I was convinced that my best and healthiest option was to forgive. . . .Victim families . . . who retain a vindictive mind-set ultimately give the offender another victim. Embittered, tormented, enslaved by the past, the quality of life is diminished. However justified, our unforgiveness undoes us. Anger, hatred, resentment, bitterness, revenge—they are death-dealing spirits, and they "will take our lives." . . . I believe the only way we can be whole, healthy, happy persons is to learn to forgive. (155-156)

This discussion on changing your attitudes may help you view life in a new light. Instead of seeing everything in a cold, critical way, you begin to see that it is possible to soften your perspective and see experiences in a way that is less abrasive. This process of inner change can be taken to a deeper level through practice of Loving Kindness Meditation.

Loving Kindness Meditation

This form of meditation facilitates a profound change in the way we view others and ourselves. The training is based on the principle that thoughts brought into a concentrated mind leave strong imprints in consciousness and thus affect future thoughts and behavior. In other words, if we think positive thoughts while the mind is concentrated, those thoughts will influence our attitudes and responses to experiences. This principle can be used in various ways to achieve various goals. In this case, we will use it to sow the seeds of friendliness, kindness, and compassion in the mind so that we can bring these qualities into our interpersonal relationships.

Though this form of practice is often referred to as Loving Kindness Meditation, it would be more accurate to call it Loving Kindness Contemplation, because it involves intentionally arousing specific thoughts and feelings while in a meditative state. We practice it in a formal and systematic way much as we did Mindfulness of Breathing. In fact, we usually start a Loving Kindness Meditation period by practicing Mindfulness of Breathing to help calm and focus the mind.

A state of focus and concentration such as that which we arouse during Mindfulness of Breathing is critical because the seeds we sow during Loving Kindness Meditation are only as powerful and effective as the concentration which supports them. If the mind is noisy and busy with other thoughts, whatever positive thoughts we try to establish will have very little impact. But once the mind is quiet and clear, we can focus full attention on the positive thoughts so that they arouse corresponding positive feelings. When such feelings are aroused, the positive thoughts penetrate deeply into our psyches.

To illustrate this point, imagine trying to make yourself heard in a room full of people who are all talking loudly. Whatever you say in that situation only adds more noise. However, if you are able to make everybody in the room quiet and gain their attention, then what you say will be easily heard.

Having established the mind in a state of peace and clarity, we proceed with Loving Kindness Meditation by intentionally bringing the following three factors into the mind:

- the positive seed thoughts
- the corresponding positive feelings
- the image of the person to whom we are directing the positive thoughts and feelings

Let us consider each factor individually.

Positive Seed Thoughts

Loving Kindness Meditation is not like mantra meditation, in which you simply repeat certain phrases over and over in the mind. Instead, you use a minimum amount of thinking—just enough to make a positive suggestion—in order to arouse the feelings of caring, kindness, and compassion. Sincerely and with full attention, you bring thoughts such as "May I be happy" or "May she be happy and well" into the mind so that they resound and stimulate a feeling of kindness. You may choose any simple, positive phrase for use in Loving Kindness Meditation, as long as it resonates in your mind and helps generate the appropriate feeling.

The Corresponding Positive Feelings

The Loving Kindness Meditation is only effective in changing your attitudes when the seed thoughts actually arouse positive feelings in the mind. Thus, when you think "May he be happy and well," you need to feel kindness and caring for the person. If you find it difficult to acknowledge or express your feelings, as many of us do, then you may be challenged by this meditation. However, we all have the capacity to feel kindness and compassion if we simply open the door and let those feelings in. Opening the door requires that you temporarily suspend your critical faculty and recognize that all human beings have similar feelings and similar vulnerabilities. The following verse from Buddhist scriptures can help you remember this truth:

> All beings tremble before violence.
> All fear death.
> All love life.
> See yourself in others.
> Then whom can you hurt?
> What harm can you do?
> (*The Dhammapada*, translated by Thomas Byrom, 36)

To help you generate a feeling of kindness and compassion, you might bring to mind an image of a helpless and vulnerable living being, such as a kitten so small that it fits into the palm of your hand. Think of the kitten looking at you with big, liquid eyes. Allow your feelings of wishing to protect and care for the kitten to arise spontaneously.

A mother nursing her child often feels this quality of protective caring, extreme tenderness, and love. These feelings are integral parts of human nature, and they easily surface when we open our hearts. Once we recognize how easily feelings of warmth, caring, and kindness can arise, it will be possible for us to bring them to consciousness during Loving Kindness Meditation.

The feelings we are trying to arouse are not romantic emotions, but rather benevolent and altruistic in nature. That is why I used the examples of a helpless kitten and a nursing baby to illustrate these feelings rather than the love felt between a man and a woman. This is not to say that the love between men and women cannot be benevolent or altruistic, but only that it is usually a more complicated emotion and therefore less appropriate for this type of contemplation.

Now that you have aroused positive feelings through a few seed thoughts, it is time to direct those feelings toward some person in particular.

The Image of the Person

When practicing Loving Kindness Meditation, you can direct the positive feelings either to specific individuals whom you know personally or, in a more general way, towards all the people around you.

The traditional approach is to begin by directing thoughts and feelings of kindness towards yourself. To many Westerners, this part of the practice seems strange because they confuse the act of being kind to themselves with being selfish. However, a feeling of kindness is radically different from a selfish state of mind. In fact if you observe the mind when it is experiencing selfishness, you will not find any real caring or kindness there. A selfish mind is in an agitated and negative state and is neither peaceful nor benevolent.

Many wise teachers say that unless we can feel loving kindness towards ourselves, it will not be possible to extend similar feelings towards others. As has been mentioned, most of us are extremely critical by nature, and this judgmental tendency is part of the reason we are so easily irritated and annoyed by human failings. Of course, no one is closer to us than we ourselves are. We live with ourselves everyday, and our critical mind sees the faults, flaws, and failings in each of our words and actions. This critical faculty can be quite merciless. Such excessive self-criticism leads to feelings of low self-esteem, poor self-image, and a lack of confidence. Taking the time to change an overly critical view of ourselves to a more caring and compassionate one is essential to our sense of well-being. Practicing the Loving Kindness Meditation beginning with ourselves can help us achieve this goal.

In order to arouse a feeling of kindness toward ourselves, we must suspend judgments about how "good" or "bad" we are. Instead, we see ourselves as vulnerable human beings in need of kindness. The feeling of a mother toward her child is not dependent upon whether the child is "worthy" of her kindness and care. When we intentionally suspend our critical faculty and open our hearts to our own vulnerabilities, a similar feeling of unconditional warmth, caring, and kindness can arise towards ourselves.

Using simple seed thoughts such as "May I be happy and well," we arouse kind feelings and direct them toward ourselves with a peaceful and concentrated mind. By repeating the seed thoughts as often as necessary, we try to sustain that quality of loving kindness toward ourselves for a while.

Having devoted some time to ourselves, we can begin to direct the same feelings of kindness toward other people on an individual basis. While we can include anybody we know in our contemplation, it is best to begin with people towards whom we already have positive feelings. As we develop skill with this contemplation, the power of the positive feelings becomes stronger, and we are better able to invite people with whom we may have difficulties into our sphere of kindness. Working gradually in this way, it will eventually be possible to feel kindness toward people we do not like or with whom we disagree. Liking, we will find, is not a prerequisite for kindness!

When we wish to direct our Loving Kindness Meditation towards an individual, we simply arouse a general image of the person in our mind. There is no need to visualize detailed features; we need only to have that person in mind as a focus for our feelings of well-wishing and kindness. For example, if someone says, "Think of an apple," we immediately have a general image of an apple in the mind. In a similar way, we can easily bring to mind the recipient of our contemplation.

It is also possible to practice Loving Kindness Meditation in a more expansive way. In this case, we repeat seed thoughts such as "May all beings be happy and well," generate a feeling of goodwill within a peaceful mind, and radiate that feeling in all directions to encompass everyone. Once again, with practice, the scope and power of the positive feelings we generate will grow and cover an expanding sphere.

Through Loving Kindness Meditation we can radically change the way we view others and ourselves. Moreover, practicing this meditation weakens the power of anger at its root cause. Rather than always seeing the glass as half empty, we begin to see that it is half full. Thus we will naturally be more patient, tolerant, and forgiving, which will result in a more peaceful and harmonious life.

E X E R C I S E :
L O V I N G   K I N D N E S S   M E D I T A T I O N

To develop your practice of Loving Kindness Meditation, try the following exercise for a period of twenty minutes. If you wish, you can use different seed thoughts to help arouse the feeling of kindness in your mind. Also, you will need to decide who to include in your contemplation and how long you will focus upon each person. Choose the approach that works best for you.

Begin the meditation period by practicing relaxation and Mindfulness of Breathing for about five minutes to help calm and focus the mind.

Once the mind is relatively quiet, let go of the breath, and bring your attention to the body sitting still. Try to arouse a feeling of warmth and caring for the body with the thought, "May I be healthy and free from all tension." Your body is vulnerable and subjected to many critical judgments and demands. Putting the critical faculty aside, try to see that the body is in need of warmth, kindness, and caring. With the thought, "May I be healthy and well," flood the whole body with a feeling of kindness. Try to sustain this feeling toward the body for a while, using the seed thoughts now and then to reinforce the feeling and help focus the mind.

If you have an ailment in any part of the body, you may want to pay special attention to that area. Using the seed thoughts, "May I be healthy and free from this ailment," direct the mind to soothe and heal that part of the body with a feeling of caring.

Having given attention to the body, now try to suffuse everything that constitutes you as a person with a feeling of warmth. Abandoning all judgment, try to consider yourself in the same way a mother would consider her only child. With the seed thought, "May I be happy and well," arouse a feeling of unconditional kindness and enfold your whole being in it. Occasionally repeating the seed thoughts, try to sustain this caring feeling toward yourself for a while.

Now you can begin to direct your feelings of kindness toward other individuals. Bring to mind someone who is important in your life. See that person smiling and, in your mind, smile back. Reach out and embrace that person with a feeling of caring and kindness using seed thoughts such as "May you be happy and well." Generate a warm feeling and completely surround this person with kindness for a while. Mentally repeat the seed thoughts as necessary to reinforce the feeling or refocus the mind.

Then let that person go, bring to mind someone else, such as a family member or a coworker, and repeat the same procedure for directing loving kindness to that person for some time. You can systematically bring to mind a number of people with whom you share your life in one way or another.

If you know someone who is ill, you may want to incorporate that person in your contemplation. Bring the ill person to mind, and reach out to touch the person with a feeling of caring and warmth. With the thought, "May you be healthy and free from this illness," radiate from your whole being a feeling of well-wishing and focus it on the person in your mind. Bathe that person in a soothing and healing energy, occasionally repeating the seed thoughts to strengthen the feeling.

When you have covered all the people you want to include in your contemplation, bring your attention back to yourself. Be happy and at peace within yourself. Be at peace with everything and everyone all around. Be at peace in the present.

Question Time

I can accept that being angry is not a pleasant experience and that anger may not be the best motivator, but it seems to be part of our natural make-up. Isn't it natural to feel angry at times?

Yes, it is perfectly "natural" to feel angry. In fact, everything that comes into existence is natural in the sense that nature allows that form of expression to manifest. Everything that has ever been felt, thought, said, or done has been perfectly natural. Nature allows for the existence of good and bad, holy and evil, beneficial and harmful, constructive and destructive: the whole gamut of possibilities.

However, it is up to us to decide which aspects of nature are worth developing and which are to be avoided. Although we cannot control everything, we do have the free will to choose what path to follow in life—the path to peace or the path to misery. If we have sufficient awareness and concentration, we can claim our right to freedom by choosing how to respond to any situation. It is natural to feel angry, but

it is also natural to feel kindness and compassion.
Which do we wish to cultivate?

If we develop an attitude of kindness as you encourage, won't other people take advantage of us?

Being kind and compassionate does not mean being
weak, gullible, or foolish. We do not abandon those
faculties of wisdom and understanding that enable us to
choose the best course of action in any situation.
Developing kindness also requires that we are kind to
ourselves by caring for our mental and physical well-
being. Thus, while we do not want to harm others, neither will we allow others to harm us.

*It seems that in order to do the right thing, I cannot always be compassion-
ate. If my children act up, I need to discipline them. Otherwise, they will not
learn to be responsible human beings. What light can you shed on this dilemma?*

The dilemma exists only if you think that being kind
means giving immediate gratification to others or yourself. True kindness, rather, is a benevolent attitude that
is concerned with the well-being of others, not just
with their immediate gratification.

For example, say you have a friend who loves choco-late, but is allergic to it. What would be the compas-sionate thing for you to do if you saw your friend about to eat some chocolate? If you were really concerned for your friend's well-being, you would probably say some-thing like, "Don't have that chocolate; let's have some ice cream instead."

Since you have your children's well-being in mind, you give them the love, support, and guidance they need to help them through life. Of course you have to discipline them at times, but that, too, comes from compassion.

When practicing Loving Kindness Meditation, if we focus our mind on some-one, will that person actually be affected by our thoughts?

That will depend upon the power of the thoughts. As I have said, the power of the mind may be greater than we realize, and we must be open to all of its possibili-ties. However, whether or not another person is affect-ed by our positive thoughts, by developing such thoughts, we definitely cultivate a positive attitude that affects the way we think, speak, and act. Everybody with whom we come into contact will benefit from this change.

As the Buddhist scriptures put it:

> We are what we think.
> All that we are arises with our thoughts.
> With our thoughts, we make the world.
> Speak or act with a pure mind
> And happiness will follow you
> As your shadow, unshakable.
> (*The Dhammapada*, translated by Thomas Byrom, 1-2)

CHAPTER ELEVEN

SELF-AWARENESS

WHILE EXPLORING THE VARIOUS ASPECTS OF the Meditative Path, we have gradually traveled a full circle. At the start of the journey, I explained that meditation involves growth in three areas: getting to know the mind, training the mind, and freeing the mind. I also noted that these three aspects of practice constitute a single process of inner exploration, discovery, and development, because progress made in one area automatically promotes growth in the other two.

Thus, as we begin observing the mind and becoming familiar with its habits, we are able to start training the mind by establishing some awareness and concentration. The development of these qualities automatically frees the mind from excessive restlessness and agitation. Then, as awareness and concentration grow in strength, we can investigate our emotions and mental states more carefully, leading to deeper insights. The new understanding that results from these insights provides opportunities for change, such as freeing the mind from negative habits. A free mind can more easily achieve refined levels of meditation and further insights. Thus the Meditative Path is a cumulative process that spirals toward more profound experiences of peace, understanding, and freedom.

A good image for the Meditative Path is a winding trail leading from the base of a mountain up to its peak. While walking in the forested area at the foot of the mountain, our view is limited. However, as we continue to follow the path winding its way around the mountain, we gradually rise above the obstructions of the valley so that our view becomes more clear and expansive. Of course, if we keep walking, we eventually reach the summit, from which we have clear and unobstructed vision of the whole panorama.

At present, you may not be close to reaching the summit in your practice of mental cultivation. But you are in position to broaden the scope of your investigation. Having explored how awareness and concentration can be used to examine reactions to pain and other unpleasant experiences, you now understand the process of investigation. This same approach of directing the light of awareness to illuminate your subjective experience of the world can be employed to investigate many other feelings, emotions, and mental states. This chapter explores a more general practice of self-observation that leads to greater self-discovery and understanding.

KNOWING YOURSELF

As aspects of the Meditative Path, self-observation and self-discovery are not exercises in self-analysis achieved through critical thinking. Rather, they are practices of direct observation through intuitive seeing and understanding of ourselves. Instead of *thinking* about life, the world, and ourselves, we use self-awareness to *observe* how experiences affect us on a subjective level of feelings and emotions and to discover how we habitually react to such experiences.

Although in the course of our lives we may learn much about the world outside us, that knowledge is less essential to our happiness than what we learn and understand about ourselves. The following story illustrates that self-understanding is, in fact, the only knowledge that ultimately matters:

A professor from a prestigious university had been invited to give a lecture in a nearby city. To get to his destination, the professor had to cross a wide river, so he paid a peasant to row him across in a small boat. While sitting in the boat, the professor looked up at the stars in the night sky and casually asked the peasant, "My good man, have you studied astronomy?"

The poor peasant did not even know the meaning of the word astronomy, and so he humbly replied, "No sir, I don't believe I have."

Feeling a degree of contempt, the professor said, "Then you have wasted a good portion of your life." After a period of silence, the professor, unable to restrain himself, spoke again to the peasant. "Well then, my good man, are you familiar with the great works of literature?"

The peasant who had never learned to read had to admit that he didn't know anything about literature.

The professor, now quite disgusted by the peasant's ignorance, said with arrogance, "Indeed, you have wasted much of your life!"

Shortly afterwards, as they neared the middle of the fast-flowing river, the boat sprang a leak. While taking his coat off, the peasant looked at the professor and asked, "Sir, do you know how to swim?"

"No," the professor replied in a terrified whisper.

"Then, sir, I am afraid that you have wasted your entire life, because the boat is sinking!"

As this story illustrates, our ability to "swim" through the deep waters of self-understanding and self-discovery is the most important kind of knowledge we can have.

Basic Requirements for Self Knowledge

The process of self-discovery requires that we remain attentive to what we are experiencing and how it is affecting us emotionally. It involves a careful and honest observation of what motivates us to react and relate to life the way we do. Through self-discovery we clearly see and fully acknowledge our feelings, emotions, and mental states. This investigative process leads to insight and wisdom.

At this stage of practice, everything in life, whether pleasant or unpleasant, should be viewed as "grist for the mill" of awareness and as a subject for our meditative reflection. Seen in this way, every situation and encounter provides an opportunity for learning more about our strengths and weaknesses, and problems in life become sources of insight and understanding.

Success in the practice of self-discovery requires three essential qualities:

- self-awareness: the ability to objectify and observe clearly what you are experiencing and feeling
- complete honesty: the desire to know and understand yourself without pretense or fear
- time and interest: the time to consider your inner world carefully so that insights can arise

Let's look more closely at each of these factors.

Self-Awareness

A good portion of this book has been devoted to describing the nature of awareness and how it can be developed and put to use. Indeed, we could say that self-awareness is the only way to arrive at insight and wisdom. In order to understand ourselves, we need to be attentive to our inner world, observing our feelings and listening to our emotions. Self-awareness makes this attention and observation possible. The practice of self-discovery involves the application of these qualities during all aspects of life.

For example, when someone praises you, what do you feel? How do you react? How is this experience different from what you experience when someone criticizes you? Questions like these involve us in a direct process of introspection and observation that reveals something about the mind and its tendencies. Self-awareness is simply the ability to keep the light of observation turned on so that we can see what is happening in the mind and thus discover more about ourselves.

Complete Honesty

In order to see what is happening within us, we need not

only the light of awareness, but also the sincere desire to know who we are and what we feel. This desire implies a willingness to abandon all pretense or excuses and, with complete honesty and humility, acknowledge what we are feeling and thinking. We must leave behind concern for what we "should be" feeling, or any preoccupation with justifying our reactions. Rather, we want to know for ourselves directly and honestly "What am I feeling, and why am I feeling this way?" This knowledge requires that we stand completely naked in the light of self-awareness.

Unfortunately, many of us are not ready or able to acknowledge fully our true feelings. Often, our preoccupation with presenting a certain image or personality to the outside world distances us from the way we really feel. As we invest more time and energy into portraying this or that type of person, we increasingly lose the ability to see ourselves as we are. In the worst case, we become actors who have forgotten that they are acting.

Consider, for instance, a person who has always been the "strong" member of a family, providing support and leadership for everyone else. In any difficult situation, such as a case of serious illness or loss in the family, that strong person will automatically assume the stoic role. Unfortunately, this often means that the person will not acknowledge his or her own feelings of grief. These feelings will remain unresolved and possibly lead to other feelings, such as depression.

Fear is another obstacle that can block the honest acknowledgment of feelings and emotions. Because we feel threatened by them, we are often afraid to allow our feelings to become fully conscious. We are especially afraid of acknowledging negative feelings, such as jealousy, envy, resentment, and insecurity. Many of us consider these negative feelings to be personal failings and resist admitting that we experience them, even to ourselves. For instance, we often hide our true feelings when a coworker gets a raise or a promotion. Often, these unacknowledged feelings of envy and resentment turn inward against ourselves, where they manifest as low self-esteem or even self-hatred. We also deny positive feelings. For example, fully acknowledging that you care for another person may be sometimes very difficult, because you fear rejection and the possibility of being hurt.

This fear of self-knowing can exist at different levels. At deeper levels, we may be completely unaware of how our fear is influencing us. However, through self-awareness we can recognize the ordinary forms of fear and gradually overcome this obstacle to self-discovery. It is only necessary that our desire for self-knowledge be greater than the fear of seeing something that we may not like in ourselves. I have found two reflections to be very helpful in promoting the desire for understanding and the courage to acknowledge what we are feeling.

First, it is helpful to recognize that no one is all good or all bad and that most of us are a mixture of positive and negative tendencies. We do not need to exaggerate our negative feelings or thoughts or give them the power to intimidate us. Rather than cowering in the dark, we shine the light of awareness onto our perceived faults or flaws. When we do, we often see that they are not very serious after all. Their power to haunt us comes from our fear. Having negative feelings or thoughts does not mean that we must act upon or be slaves to them. With awareness and understanding, we can decide how best to deal with whatever thoughts and feelings come up.

For instance, in my life as a monk, I sometimes counseled terminally ill patients and tried to be with them when the end of life was near. One case involved a friend whom I had known for many years. He was dying of cancer, and the final few days were very difficult for him. As I sat by his bedside through the night, I found myself wishing that he would die quickly. What shocked me was that this wish was not coming from a desire for my friend to be free from his misery, but from me wanting to get away from the unpleasant situation. Obviously, this thought was not very noble or compassionate, but it was important that I recognize and acknowledge its existence so that I could understand my experience. Though my thought was selfish, it did not mean that I was a selfish person with no compassion for my dying friend. I was simply exhausted and needed a rest.

A second reflection worth keeping in mind is that all feelings, emotions, and mental states are transient; in other words, they come and go. Emotions and mental states are only visitors passing through the mind; none of them stay. Using the light of awareness, we can see these various visitors coming into consciousness and then leaving again. Awareness and observation help us see our feelings, emotions, and mental states as passengers on a train. Passengers get on the train, and then they get off. Some of them are nicely dressed and pleasant, while others may be untidy and coarse. But once they've gotten on the train, passengers inevitably get off again, and the train of our mental processes continues on its way.

When we use the light of awareness to illuminate both positive and negative visitors that pass through the mind, we come to recognize that no mental state or emotion is an intrinsic or permanent aspect of our true selves. Thus, feelings and reactions need not be taken personally or allowed to threaten our peace of mind. Naturally, we will not willingly welcome guests who are troublemakers, but we do not need to fear or fight them. We simply need to show them the door.

The meditation exercise at the end of this chapter gives you an opportunity to practice this reflection for yourself. For the present, let's just say that whatever we can objectify and see coming and going in the ever-moving stream of our mental processes cannot be our true self. Thus, we can fearlessly allow the light of awareness to shine into every nook and cranny, because everything that we see brings us understanding and freedom—understanding of the known and freedom from the unknown.

Time and Interest

Self-discovery is a continuously unfolding process that happens throughout your practice of the Meditative Path at various stages and in various ways. Some insights and understandings arise spontaneously during formal meditation, or even while doing ordinary things. However, these experiences are not accidental or without cause; they arise when appropriate mental conditions exist. Devoting time and interest to cultivating the Meditative Path has a cumulative effect that inevitably culminates in such experiences.

The seemingly spontaneous insights that arise as you continue to practice may be compared to fruit gradually ripening on a tree. It takes time and nutrients for fruit to ripen, but eventually, the process reaches a point when, even in the absence of any external cause, the ripe fruit simply drops to the ground.

For other insights, we may need to probe our way toward a clear understanding by applying our attention to investigating a feeling, emotion, or reaction. This investigation involves an intentional process of "tuning in" or "listening carefully" to our inner world so that we gradually allow things to become clear. This unfolding often takes time and, especially with more complicated emotions, may involve working through many layers of feelings.

CULTIVATING SELF-KNOWLEDGE

Although we could subject every experience and reaction to careful investigation, we do not need to investigate everything. We simply bring awareness into our lives so that we can be more sensitive to what is happening in the present. Most particularly, we notice what we experience within ourselves, our reactions to the outside world, and how our words and deeds affect the world around us. While there is inner peace and outer harmony, it is sufficient for us to know that everything is going well. Unfortunately, life is not all smooth sailing and, if we remain aware, sooner or later we will notice some waves or disruption to the peace and harmony. These are occasions when we should look closely at our experiences and see what is happening, both within and around us.

In other words, when there is a problem, we should take the time and have the interest to direct our awareness to investigate the experience carefully so that understanding can arise and a resolution can be achieved. In some situations, the nature of the disturbance will be easily seen and understood. Other circumstances may require a great deal of patient and careful contemplation in order to arrive at a better understanding.

The insights and knowledge that arise from self-investigations vary in nature and significance. Sometimes, the clear understanding of a problem brings immediate resolution. At other times, the insights reveal aspects of ourselves that need to be addressed and worked through before a problem can be resolved effectively. It is best not to place too many restrictions on how a process of self-discovery might unfold. We simply watch and learn and thus move toward greater peace and harmony.

A Mother's Grief

The liberating effect of clear and insightful understanding is illustrated by a powerful story from ancient India:

A mother could not accept that her only child had died of an illness. Carrying her dead child in her arms, the distraught mother visited various doctors and spiritual teachers, begging for medicine to revive her child. When she approached the Buddha with her request, he told her that he would gladly give her the medicine she sought. But first, he told her, she must bring him a teaspoon of mustard seeds from a household in which there had never been a death.

The mother ran to the nearest village and went from house to house. Although everyone she asked was willing to give her the teaspoon of mustard seeds, she could not find a single household in which there had never been a death.

Finally, the realization and understanding pierced through her denial, and she acknowledged the reality of her child's death. Indeed, she realized the universality of death and the truth that everyone who is born will eventually die. Though she still grieved the death of her child, the distress and anguish caused by her denial vanished as a result of her realization.

This dramatic story teaches us two valuable lessons. First, living in denial causes us mental stress, anxiety, and fear. In order to free the mind from such oppression, we must recognize and come to terms with the basic nature of the human condition. Only when we fully acknowledge our own mortality and the uncertainty and insecurity of life can we free ourselves from fear and anxiety.

Second, the story illustrates the important role of a good teacher. Many people had told the mother that her child was

dead, but they could not penetrate her denial. Her mind needed to be guided to a point where that knowledge could arise
from a direct realization. Often a good teacher, or a good counselor for that matter, provides the opportunity for students to
see the truth for themselves by pointing them in the right direction.

The lesson learned by the mother in this traditional
Buddhist story is central to the peaceful resolution of many
kinds of less tragic life problems, as I also experienced for
myself during my years in the forest monasteries in Thailand
where I lived and trained.

Conditions at one monastery were very austere, and the
monks who lived there experienced a lot of physical hardship.
We would awaken at 3 A.M. for meditation and chanting, eat
one meal a day in the morning, and often work all afternoon. In
the evening, we would meet in an open pavilion for more meditation, after which the teacher gave a talk based upon some
aspect of the monk's training.

One evening, we had been sitting on the hard floor for
many hours. My legs were aching badly, and I felt very tired and
very hungry. The teacher's talk seemed to go on forever, and as
we continued to sit in the open air, the mosquitoes had a feast.
Slowly, without my being fully aware of it, my mind filled with
negative feelings and thoughts of aversion toward the teacher,

the mosquitoes, the pain, and everything else I was experiencing. Even though I continued to sit quietly, inside I felt like a volcano ready to erupt.

I was really miserable. Then a moment of self-awareness arose, and I looked closely and carefully to see what was really causing the suffering. As I examined my mind under the light of awareness, it became clear that, while my physical situation was uncomfortable, it was by no means unbearable. What was really making my mind miserable were thoughts and feelings that took me out of the present and made me want my situation to be other than it was. I realized that though I could have tried to change the external conditions, I could more easily change my thinking.

As soon as I stopped the process of "wanting this and not wanting that," my mind experienced immediate peace. The volcano inside me transformed into a pool of cool water. Though the external conditions were the same, my internal experience changed radically. By seeing clearly and understanding the source of my mental suffering, I was able to move out of suffering and into a renewed sense of emotional equanimity.

The Future Is Uncertain

The following personal experience illustrates how we can apply awareness to gradually make a feeling more fully conscious so that understanding and resolution can be achieved.

It is possible for monks to leave the Buddhist order, but leaving is not to be done lightly. By the fifth year of my monastic training, I was feeling quite comfortable and confident in my vocation. However, toward the end of that year, which marked the completion of my formal training period under my teacher, I started to feel anxious. At first this anxiety was very subtle, and I could not identify what I was feeling or why. I was simply aware of a persistent, vague, uneasy feeling in the back of my mind.

As the days passed, I tried to "tune in" to my feeling by quietly and gently directing my attention to it. Gradually, the feeling became clear and crystallized into consciousness. My anxiety and trepidation was, I came to realize, associated with the uncertainty of my future. My dilemma was formed out of the following train of thoughts: "Being a monk feels fine now, but how will I feel when I am sixty-five? Will I regret having taken this path? I need to be sure that I am making the right choice. How can I be sure?" Basically, I wanted a guarantee about the future, and because no guarantee was possible, my anxiety grew.

Of course, as this pattern of thinking and feeling became clear in my mind, the solution to the dilemma was obvious. When I came to terms with the fact that any future was uncertain, my anxiety simply dissolved away.

We all fall prey to anxiety, fear, and insecurity when we fail to fully acknowledge and accommodate ourselves to the fact that the future is uncertain. However, we need not live with fear or anxiety in the present. Through understanding, we realize that the only way to prepare for the future is by living wisely in the present.

Thich Nhat Hanh has crystallized this realization in his translation of the following wise words of advice from a traditional Buddhist text:

Do not pursue the past.
Do not lose yourself in the future.
The past no longer is.
The future has not yet come.
Looking deeply at life as it is
In the very here and now,
The practitioner dwells
In stability and freedom.
(*Our Appointment with Life*, 5)

Praise and Blame

Among the situations we face in daily life, experiences of praise and blame provide the most fruitful opportunity for practicing self-understanding and self-discovery. We are all praised at times and blamed or criticized at others. Naturally, it is pleasing to receive praise, but should our self-worth and self-esteem be determined by praise alone? Should the possibility of criticism weigh heavily on our minds? Turning the light of awareness on our experiences of praise and blame can teach us much about how our mental processes contribute to inner misery and inner peace.

In Thai culture, calling someone a "dog" is extremely offensive. My teacher used this example to illustrate an important truth: "If somebody calls you a dog," he would tell us, "stop and look around at your behind. If you see a tail there, then that person was correct. However, if you see no tail, you know that you are not a dog and that the person who called you a dog was just talking nonsense. Either way, once you understand the truth of the matter, you will not be upset by that person's comment."

In other words, there is no need to react with anger or fear when we encounter criticism. Through observation and understanding, we can accommodate the fact that we will inevitably encounter some criticism. When it comes our way, we can reflect on that experience. Of course, being criticized is not pleasant, but do we want to give it the power to make us miserable? Isn't it better to stop and consider whether the criticism is valid? If the criticism is not valid, there is no need to bother about it. If the criticism is valid and there really is a tail back there, then we should be prepared to accept responsibility for our actions and to take steps to make amends if we can.

Conversely, if we are told that we are "the light of the world," it may be worth looking in the mirror to see whether we are really shining. In other words, praise should also be considered for its validity and should not determine our self-worth. With self-awareness and understanding, we can learn to live with praise and blame without becoming a victim of either.

UNRESOLVED EMOTIONS

Each of us has had experiences that are forgotten or only vaguely remembered. It is not uncommon that, as a result of meditation, some of these forgotten memories become fully conscious. When these memories are associated with important past events, they can arouse strong feelings and emotions in the mind. Depending upon the nature of the event, the feelings can be strongly positive or negative. Positive feelings include deep gratitude, compassion, and love, while common negative feelings include remorse, anger, fear, and grief.

Especially in the case of negative feelings or emotions, it is important to deal with them in a way that brings resolution and peace to the mind. We are often able to accomplish this by ourselves. However, in the case of traumatic experiences involving complex emotions, it is sometimes better to seek guidance from a good teacher or counselor. For instance, in the course of practice, one of my students was overwhelmed by memories of sexual abuse. Obviously, such a complex emotional and psychological issue required the guidance of a knowledgeable professional whose skill could help the student work through such feelings.

I bring up this case to make the point that the practice of self-discovery through meditation is not intended to be a form of therapy for treating serious emotional or psychological problems. I personally believe that a skilled therapist can provide a more direct and effective approach to resolving such issues. However, meditation can often be a valuable part of the therapy.

The Process of Self-Discovery

I hope that the preceding discussion has given you some appreciation for the process of self-discovery. Remember that this aspect of practice is not a matter of following a formal technique or method. It is a more intuitive process, much like creating a piece of art. There are helpful guidelines for pointing the mind in the right direction, but insights must be allowed to unfold in a natural way.

You may be wondering whether there is an end to this process. What is that completely unobstructed vision from the summit of the mountain? All true spiritual paths, but not necessarily all institutionalized religions, have as their goal the realization of a transcendental and absolute truth or reality. Of course, various traditions call that one reality by different names and point to it in different ways. But by its very nature, this truth is beyond the limitations of concepts and descriptions. Furthermore, if it is the Truth, then it cannot belong to anyone. It simply is. However, it is possible for the sincere seeker to realize this Truth and come to embody it.

Traditional Buddhist texts equate this ultimate Truth with "supreme happiness" and emphatically assert its reality:

> There is an unborn, an uncreated, an unconditioned. Here there is no coming, no going, no standing, no ceasing, no beginning; it has no basis, no evolution, no support; it is the end of all suffering. (paraphrased from *Udana* VIII, verses 1-4)

In his study of various spiritual paths, Wayne Teasdale suggests that realizing this Truth may indeed be the common goal of all spirituality:

> Finally, in mystical experiences, we are touched by something ultimate, by a mystery that takes us to tran-

scendental realms, . . . the "place" of the totality, the
source. (*The Mystic Heart*, 71)

However, none can grant this experience to us. We must
each realize it for ourselves.

EXERCISE: WHO AM I?

You will find this meditation exercise to be quite different
from anything presented so far. It is based on the teachings of
the famous Indian master, Sri Ramana Maharshi. His system of
introspection involves meditating on the question "Who am I?"
With a quiet and focused mind, we raise the question "Who am
I?" as a means of turning the mind deeply inward toward the
source of that question. Before explaining in detail how to practice this meditation, I wish to share the experience of a student
who was using this method.

This student told me that while meditating, his mind had
reached a level of calmness. As he posed the question "Who am
I?" he sensed a very soft answer deep within. He focused his
attention more carefully and posed the question again. This
time, the answer seemed closer, but it was still not clear. Ever so
gently and carefully, he directed his mind to the question with

complete sincerity. Then, out of the silence in his mind, he heard the answer, "Who wants to know?"

The purpose of this exercise is to help you recognize what is "not you" and to point the mind toward silent knowing. It is based upon the premise that what you can objectify and witness arising in consciousness and then disappearing cannot be a permanent part of who you are. For instance, all sensory experiences arise and pass away. Likewise, thoughts and feelings are transient and continually changing. To the extent that you can be aware of these thoughts, feelings, and sensations coming and going in consciousness, you realize that none of them can really be you.

Naturally, questions arise: "Who is it that knows these objects and experiences? If I am not the visitor, then am I the host? Who am I? What am I? Where am I?"

Meditators in many traditions have struggled to answer these questions. Here is how Zen Master Bassui Tokusho described this practice:

> However much you try through logical reasoning and definition to know your original face before your birth or your original home, you are doomed to failure.
>
> Even if you search the core of your being, becoming full of questioning, you won't find anything that you could call a personal mind or essence.

Yet when someone calls your name, something in you hears and responds. Find out who it is! Find out now!

(Timothy Freke, *Zen Wisdom*, 27)

In this meditation exercise, we pose such a question as "Who am I?" to the quiet mind to turn toward that quality of knowing. The intention is to go beyond superficial concepts and thoughts and approach the source from which they arise. However, to practice this subtle form of introspection successfully requires that that mind be reasonably peaceful and able to focus. The best way to experiment with this practice is to do it for a short time, about five to ten minutes, during your normal meditation period.

Practice Mindfulness of Breathing for a while until the mind is calm. Then let the breath go and turn your attention to the silence in the mind. Quietly listening, gently and with interest, pose the question "Who am I?" to the mind. Listen carefully to the question. Where is it coming from?

Whatever comes out of the silence is an object of the knowing. That object arises and passes away, so it cannot be you. Even the question "Who am I?" arises and passes away, but who is asking that question? Gently keep turning the attention back toward the source and ask, "Who am I?"

When the mind is distracted by thoughts, simply bring it back to the source by asking the question "Who is thinking?" If you begin to feel confused by the process, cut through that confusion and go directly to the source by asking "Who is confused?"

Each time you pose such a question, the mind is turned back toward the silent knowing from which all concepts are born. Go into that silence and gently probe, asking "Who is this knowing?"

With sincere interest, delicate attention, and gentle patience, direct the mind to the task of inquiry for as long as you feel appropriate. Then return to Mindfulness of Breathing for the rest of your meditation period.

QUESTION TIME

Well, what is the answer? Who am I, and who is it that knows?

If we could arrive at that insight simply by being told, we would all surely be enlightened by now. Unfortunately, even the wisest teacher can only tell us what we are not. We are not the thoughts, feelings, sensory experiences, and all other things that arise and pass away in consciousness. Of course, every concept of self, from the simplest to the most exalted, arises and passes away in the mind, and so none of them can be the true answer to the question "Who am I?" Knowing what we are not, we are now left with the task of discovering the truth beyond concept. As this paradox is expressed by the Zen Master Dosan:

> Wherever I go,
> There he is.
> He is no other than myself
> But I am not him.
> (Timothy Freke, *Zen Wisdom*, 87)

You have indicated that the practice of self-discovery through meditation is not intended to address serious emotional or psychological issues. Are there any mental problems for which practicing meditation could actually be counter-productive?

Training the mind is not easy, even when it is in a so-called "normal state." People with serious emotional or psychological problems will usually find it very difficult to practice meditation.

From experience I have learned that it is not advisable for people with schizophrenia or similar conditions to practice a lot of meditation. While doing the relaxation exercise and the occasional short meditation may be useful, long periods of introspection or meditation tends to exacerbate such conditions. Other forms of training, such as Hatha Yoga and Tai Chi, which have less emphasis on introspection, may be more appropriate for some individuals. In any case, they should first seek the counsel of a wise teacher or a mental health professional.

Are there areas in which meditation and psychology overlap and can support each other?

Both meditation and psychology are concerned with studying the mind and developing mental well-being, but at very different levels.

Meditation is primarily concerned with exploring and studying the so-called normal states of mind to cultivate more refined levels of awareness, concentration, and wisdom. This work has the goal of achieving much higher levels of peace and happiness. In other words, it is a process of raising the ordinary, normal human mind to higher levels of refinement and enlightenment.

Here it should be noted that being ordinary or normal does not refer to a particular type of person. Rather, it suggests that the person is able to function, relate to, and respond to life in ways that are acceptable to society. This person has sufficient self-awareness to undertake the type of training described in this book and to cultivate the qualities mentioned above.

Psychology and psychiatry, in contrast, are fields of study developed especially to help people who are not functioning easily within that so-called normal range due to an emotional or psychological condition. Their goal is to employ various forms of therapy, counseling, and medication to help relieve the condition causing the problem so that patients can experience ordinary levels of well-being and live more normal lives.

Both meditation and psychology serve very valuable roles in our quest for mental well-being, happiness, and peace. However, neither can effectively fulfill the role of the other.

Of course, there is some overlap where these two fields of study can work together and support each other. The example I gave during the discussion of unresolved emotions is a case in point. When confronted with the difficult emotional issue of sexual abuse, it would have been very difficult for that student to make further progress in meditation without arriving at some closure or resolution. With the help of a skilled therapist, the student did that and was then able to continue cultivating the practice of meditation. In fact, this case illustrates how meditation and therapy can be used simultaneously to address a mental or emotional problem.

An example of psychology using a meditative approach is the widely used technique of "systematic desensitization," which is described as follows:

A person who suffers from anxiety works with the therapist to compile a list of feared situations, starting with those that arouse minimal anxiety and progressing to those that are the most frightening. He or she is also taught to relax deeply. Then, step-by-step, while relaxed, the person imagines the graded series of anxiety-provoking situations. The relaxation tends to inhibit any anxiety that might otherwise be elicited by the imagined scenes. The fearful person becomes able to tolerate increasingly more difficult imagined situations as he or she climbs the hierarchy over a

number of therapy sessions. This technique is useful in reducing a wide variety of fears.

(Gerald C. Davison and John M. Neale, *Abnormal
Psychology*, 48)

This technique employs many of the principles of
meditation discussed in this book, including systematic
relaxation, becoming aware of the mental process, and
gradually freeing the mind of its negative habitual tendencies.

CHAPTER TWELVE

FOLLOWING THE PATH
OF LEAST RESISTANCE

THE LAST STEP ON THE MEDITATIVE PATH IS applying what we've learned so that we can flow through life without creating unnecessary stress or problems. I call this easy way of living "following the path of least resistance." When we follow the path of least resistance, we live responsible, productive lives with meaningful goals, without sacrificing peace and harmony. Life may not be easy, but neither is it miserable. My teacher compared this way of living to "flowing water that remains still." Though this metaphor sounds like a contradiction, it is an apt way of describing the practice of flowing through life while remaining peacefully centered and not becoming a victim of circumstances or foolish thoughts.

Ideally, life should be a meditation, and meditation should be living in an enlightened way. However, before we can live in this graceful manner, we must be clear about what we want to achieve.

WHAT IS TRULY IMPORTANT IN LIFE?

The way life unfolds is neither predetermined nor accidental. Everything that arises does so only when the appropriate causes and conditions exist. Although we cannot control all the conditions under which we live, we do have free will and, to a great degree, the ability to shape life. We have the power to reflect and decide what we want to do and to discover the best way to do it.

All of us share an aspiration for happiness and fulfillment. Regardless of the direction we take, what turns we make, and where we choose to rest along the way, our decisions are born from the desire to achieve happiness. Even when we undertake a difficult task that involves hardship, we do so out of the conviction that, in some way, our undertaking will help us achieve fulfillment.

But in our quest for happiness and fulfillment, are we simply rushing along, blindly grasping at one thing after another without clearly knowing what we want? Making wise choices requires that we stop and look deeply within to identify what is truly important and valuable to us. Otherwise, we may establish goals for ourselves and strive to achieve them only to find that they are of no real significance in our quest for fulfillment.

Consider, for example, the experience of a man driven by ambition to climb Mount Everest. Although he had a family and a regular job, he devoted much of his time and energy towards achieving that goal. Finally, he had the opportunity to attempt the climb, but it did not go well. As the expedition neared the summit, the climbing party was battered by a terrible snowstorm with gale winds and subfreezing temperatures. The climbers were trapped on the side of the mountain, completely at the mercy of the elements.

Most of the climbers perished in that storm, but this man survived to recount his ordeal. He said that during those hours when death seemed certain, he thought mostly of his wife and children and regretted not having spent more time with them. It became clear to him that the really important thing in his life was not climbing Mount Everest, but his relationship with his family. Fortunately, he was given the chance to redirect his energies to align with his true values.

Only when we are clearly aware of what is meaningful in our lives can we know our goals and establish correct priorities for our limited resources of time and energy. Naturally, these priorities will change many times as we move from one stage of life to another. But if we remain continuously in touch with our values, we can regularly check to see that the goals we are striving to achieve remain congruent with them.

A balanced approach to life requires that we consider both our external goals and the equally important goals we set for our inner life. Surely, no external achievement can be meaningful unless it is supported by a set of inner accomplishments, including peace, self-knowledge, and the freedom to shape our destiny by being able to direct the mind, as the following story illustrates:

In India, many spiritual teachers are greatly venerated by their followers. A wealthy merchant visited such a spiritual teacher. When he came into the teacher's presence, the merchant threw himself on the floor and worshipped at the feet of the holy man.

The master asked, "Why do you express such extreme veneration?"

The merchant replied, "Because, Sir, you have renounced all the material wealth of this world."

On hearing this, the holy man rose from his cushion, threw himself at the feet of the merchant, and began to venerate him.

Shocked and bewildered, the merchant asked, "Sir, what are you doing?"

The master looked up at him and said, "If you worshipped me because I renounced material things, then surely I must worship you for having renounced that which is of much greater value—self-knowledge and peace!"

The moral of this story is that in our quest for happiness, we must not sacrifice our inner well-being. Whatever else we seek, being at peace within ourselves is an integral part of achieving happiness. With this understanding, we can establish goals that are consistent with our values and then strive to realize them by following the path of least resistance.

A TURTLE WITH A MUSTACHE

Not only must our goals be true to our values, but they must also be realistic. While living in the monastery in Perth, I met a young man who was obsessed with maintaining good health. He told me that the only reason people became sick or died was that they did not believe fully in physical immortality. His goal, he told me, was to achieve physical immortality through the power of positive thinking.

After talking with this young man for a while, I realized that I had better things to do with my limited time in this life than seeking to extend it indefinitely! Striving to reach an unrealistic goal would waste my most precious resource, time to practice towards achieving the awareness, concentration, and serenity that so many meditators have achieved by following the Meditative Path.

Of course, setting realistic goals does not require that we limit ourselves to mediocre or trivial pursuits. We can strive to realize noble, grand, and inspiring things. However, what we strive for should be real, relevant, and attainable. My teacher would sometimes compare the quest for an unrealistic goal to a search for a turtle with a mustache. That search, he would say with a smile, would be long and futile.

FLOW LIKE A RIVER

Knowing our direction and having set our goals, we flow toward our destination like a river finding its way to the ocean.

Many wise teachers have offered insights into how best to make the journey through life without unnecessary inner turmoil or outer conflict. Unfortunately, there is no one secret that will be effective in every situation. Life is a continuously unfolding process of new moments of experience, each different from anything that has existed in the past or will exist in the future. Thus, the wisdom of all the sages and our own understanding gained from experiences can provide at best only guidelines and principles for living. Following the path of least resistance requires applying awareness, sensitivity, and wisdom to each present situation as it arises.

The path of least resistance is not a lazy or irresponsible way of living, nor is it a hard and tortuous process. It simply means that we do what needs to be done in order to achieve goals that are consistent with our values in ways that create the least stress. Using the skills we have gained by traveling along the Meditative Path can help us remain centered in the present, so that our intuitive wisdom can respond effectively to each situation. As the Meditative Path teaches us, the path to happiness requires

Knowing what needs to be done,
Being fully present while doing it, and
Not making a problem out of it.

As we have seen, the habit of the untrained mind is to create problems out of ordinary pleasant and unpleasant life experiences. However, it is possible for us to be free of all such unnecessary stress. By remaining awake in the present, we recognize and let go of the tendency to create problems in the mind. If the moment is pleasant, we enjoy it. If it is unpleasant, we endure it or change it. In either case, we avoid creating a problem out of anything that life brings our way.

This approach to enlightened living is succinctly expressed in the Serenity Prayer, which I prefer to paraphrase as:

May I have the courage to change what can be changed.

May I have the patience to endure what can't be changed,

And may I have the wisdom to know the difference.

The highly renowned teacher, Thich Nhat Hanh, encourages his students to maintain a "half smile" throughout the day. That is a wonderful practice to develop; but, at the very least, we should go through our days without a frown. Frowns indicate that the mind is making problems out of ordinary life experiences by getting stuck in the process of reactive thinking. Living in a reactive way is like carrying a heavy rock on our shoulders. We don't need that burden, nor do we have to continue carrying it. We can let go.

As we have learned, we can use our investigative powers to become aware of why and how we are reacting as we do and use that awareness to redirect our thinking towards letting go of the habitual reactions that stir up the mind. When we let go of these negative patterns of thinking and reacting, we put down the heavy rock and immediately experience lightness. As my teacher Ajahn Chah expressed this idea:

Do everything with a mind that lets go. Do not expect
any praise or reward. If you let go a little, you will have
a little peace. If you let go a lot, you will have a lot of
peace. If you let go completely, you will know complete
peace and freedom. Your struggles with the world will
have come to an end.

(Jack Kornfield and Paul Breiter, *A Still Forest Pool*, 73)

To follow the path of least resistance is to discover peace in
every breath and in every step, in talking and in being silent, in
action and in nonaction, in being with people and in being
alone. It is to flow through life in the peaceful way described in
this Zen poem by Ekai:

Spring flowers, autumn moon,
Summer breeze, winter snow
When the mind is free from unnecessary thoughts
Every season is just perfect!

(Timothy Freke, *Zen Wisdom*, 33)

A FINAL WORD

This book is not intended to be the final word on meditation. Its aim is to provide you with some practical guidelines for
cultivating the skills of the Meditative Path so that your life has
more inner peace and outer harmony.

From my own experience, I'd like to offer the following practical suggestions for putting what you've learned into practice:

- Establish and maintain a regular daily practice of formal meditation.

- Develop awareness around ordinary daily activities by cultivating meditation in action.

- Make time for introspection to remain in touch with your feelings and emotions.

- When there is a problem, allow it to become fully conscious in the light of awareness and use your intuitive wisdom to solve it.

- Know what is valuable in your life and establish realistic goals consistent with those values.

- Remain centered as you strive to realize your goals by utilizing the skills developed in meditation.

- Travel lightly by not burdening yourself with unnecessary external or internal activity.

- Flow like a river toward the ocean, finding the path of least resistance.

Exercise: A Day for Meditation

Once you have maintained a regular meditation practice for some time, it will be extremely beneficial for you to do a short meditation retreat. The ideal way is to participate in an organized retreat held in a quiet setting under the guidance of a teacher. However, if no such opportunity exists, you may want to try a personal half-day or day-long retreat.

This day is exclusively devoted to cultivating the Meditative Path. Therefore, everything you do has as its purpose developing awareness and peace. Of course, you may be trying to achieve these goals every day, but on this day, you will endeavor to establish more favorable conditions. For instance, you will forego work, social plans, and family responsibilities. Also, you will try not to answer the telephone, read newspapers, or listen to the radio or television. Your day for meditation is a quiet time just for yourself, a time to relax into the present, abiding in peaceful awareness and learning to let go of the usual busyness.

The following suggestions give you some idea of how to structure a day for meditation. However, you can organize the day and schedule to suit your own practice. If your meditation is progressing well, you may want to include more periods of formal meditation and eliminate some other activities:

When you awake in the morning, remember that this is your day for cultivating awareness and peace. While you are still in bed, establish awareness and center yourself by focusing on the breath for a while. Then get up and brush your teeth, wash your face, and do all your morning activities in a calm and relaxing way, cultivating awareness throughout every activity. Remain centered and try not to let the mind get lost in scattered thinking. While taking a shower, do so with the mind and body together, enjoying the shower so that by the time you have finished, you feel light and refreshed.

Before breakfast is a good time to do a period of Mindfulness of Breathing meditation for twenty to thirty minutes. Calmly arrange your seat and begin your meditation without any rush or anticipation. Enjoy the experience of being able to care for the body by gently relaxing and soothing every part. Then, with vigilant and patient effort, encourage the mind to embrace the breath and let go of all other concerns.

After the period of formal meditation, prepare breakfast for yourself in a quiet and peaceful way. Enjoy eating your breakfast, savoring each mouthful.

When thoughts arise in the mind during the day, do not let them draw you into unnecessary distraction. Remind yourself that the present is too precious to be wasted on trivial mental chatter. Just let all those thoughts fade away as you ground yourself in the now.

Having finished breakfast, wash the dishes and clean up in a calm and relaxed way, nourishing awareness through every activity.

After meals, it is usually good to do some walking meditation. You can either do a period of formal walking meditation or go for a more casual walk. Mindfully walking, peacefully walking, enjoy the walk. Later, you can do some yoga, Tai Chi, or some other form of exercise that will allow the mind to remain centered and peaceful.

Before lunch, take the opportunity to practice another period of Mindfulness of Breathing.

At lunchtime, prepare your lunch and enjoy eating it as you did breakfast. Take your time and don't rush, because this is your day.

In the afternoon, do simple chores around the house or garden for a while, developing awareness in every activity.

During the afternoon, practice Mindfulness of Breathing again and do some walking meditation.

If you wish, make tea or coffee for yourself and enjoy drinking it sitting in the garden or by a window, as in the following Zen poem:

Silently sitting by the window.

Leaves fall and flowers bloom.

The seasons come and go.

Could there be a better life?

(Timothy Freke, *Zen Wisdom*, 123)

Before dinner, try to practice another period of Mindfulness of Breathing.

Prepare and enjoy dinner in a leisurely, peaceful manner.

In the evening, you may want to go for a walk and enjoy nature. If the mind becomes noisy, gently brush the noise away and remain serene. Later, you may wish to read an inspiring article or book, listen to recorded talks on meditation, or play some soothing instrumental music.

Before bed, try a period of Loving Kindness Meditation, beginning with yourself, then including others in your sphere of peace and caring.

Having experienced a day of mindfulness, retire in comfort and sleep peacefully.

QUESTION TIME

I know what is of true value in my life, and it's not my job. Unfortunately, I have to work for a living. How do I get around that?

Although your work may not be a fulfilling aspect of your life, it provides you with a livelihood. In other words, it is a means to an end that enables you to pursue more rewarding goals. Of course, the ideal situation would be to work at a job that you find interesting and rewarding. If this is not possible, you must make the best of your situation. If you can't enjoy your work, then patiently endure it, but don't allow it to become a burden by dwelling on negative thoughts or feelings.

Earning a living is important, but how much do you really need to live comfortably? The more you "need" and the more you spend, the more you have to earn. Naturally, this usually means working long, difficult hours. Simplifying life even a little can greatly reduce the pressure on your time. Much of life is a compromise, and you must find your own balance.

Isn't spending a whole day being quiet and peaceful extremely boring?

If the mind is really quiet and peaceful, it will not be bored. On the contrary, a resting mind is joyful and happy. However, while still under the influence of the hindrances, the mind will find it difficult to maintain a meditative mood for long without becoming restless or bored. Therefore you must be patient and try to use skilful means to encourage the mind. Discover ways to help the mind slow down and enjoy resting in the present.

If a whole day seems too long for you, then begin with a half-day or a few hours. You must know yourself and practice at a level that is appropriate, but don't be afraid to challenge your mind to see what is possible.

What advice would you give to more experienced practitioners?

The same as for new ones: Keep at it!

Unfortunately, as with any other skill of training, meditation practice can deteriorate if it is neglected. This same danger exists for all meditators, even experienced ones.

Over the years, I have found two things to be very

helpful motivators for keeping up with a meditation practice. The first is having at least occasional contact with wise teachers, spiritual seekers, and other meditators. Although reading books or listening to recorded talks can also provide renewed encouragement and inspiration for practice, there is something quite special about being in the physical presence of people who are actively traveling the Meditative Path. More than what they say, it is often the quality of their being that is the source of the inspiration.

The other powerful reminder of the need for practice is solitude—those precious periods when we can withdraw our attention from the superficial noise of our busy lives and turn our gaze within, toward the source of all that we are. These occasions, even if only brief, provide us with a genuine perspective on our lives so that what is truly important becomes clear again.

As my teacher Ajahn Chah put it:

Try to be mindful, and let things take their natural course. Then your mind will become still in any surroundings, like a still forest pool. All kinds of wonderful, rare animals will come to drink at the pool, and you will clearly see the nature of all things. You will see many strange and wonderful things come and go, but you will be still. This is the happiness of the Buddha. (Jack Kornfield and Paul Breiter, *A Still Forest Pool*, vi)

Works Cited

Byrom, Thomas. *Dhammapada: The Sayings of the Buddha*. Boston: Shambhala, 1993.

Davison, Gerald C., and John M. Neale. *Abnormal Psychology*. New York: John Wiley and Sons, 1996.

Easwaran, Eknath. *The Dhammapada: Translated for the Modern Reader*. Tomales, CA: Nilgiri Press, 1996.

Freke, Timothy. *Zen Wisdom, Daily Teachings from the Zen Masters*. New York: Sterling Publishing Company, 1997.

Kornfield, Jack, and Paul Breiter. *A Still Forest Pool: The Insight Meditation of Achaan Chah*. Wheaton, IL: Theosophical Publishing House, 1985.

McDonald, Kathleen. *How to Meditate: A Practical Guide*. Boston: Wisdom, 1990.

Teasdale, Wayne. *The Mystic Heart: Discovering a Universal Spirituality in the World's Religions*. San Rafael, CA: New World Library, 1999.

Thich Nhat Hanh. *Peace in Every Step*. New York: Bantam Books, 1992.

———. *Our Appointment with Life: Discourse on Living Happily in the Present Moment*. Berkeley, CA: Parallax Press, 1990.

Tutu, Desmond. *No Future Without Forgiveness*. New York: Doubleday, 1999.

QUEST BOOKS
are published by
The Theosophical Society in America,
Wheaton, Illinois 60189-0270,
a branch of a world fellowship,
a membership organization
dedicated to the promotion of the unity of
humanity and the encouragement of the study of
religion, philosophy, and science, to the end that
we may better understand ourselves and our place in
the universe. The Society stands for complete
freedom of individual search and belief.
For further information about its activities,
write, call 1-800-669-1571, e-mail olcott@theosmail.net,
or consult its Web page: http://www.theosophical.org

*The Theosophical Publishing House
is aided by the generous support of
THE KERN FOUNDATION,
a trust established by Herbert A. Kern
and dedicated to Theosophical education.*